# JESUS
# BEFORE CHRISTIANITY

# Albert Nolan

# JESUS
# BEFORE CHRISTIANITY

ORBIS ⊕ BOOKS

Maryknoll, New York 10545

The Catholic Foreign Mission Society of America (Maryknoll) recruits and trains people for overseas missionary service. Through Orbis Books, Maryknoll aims to foster the international dialogue that is essential to mission. The books published, however, reflect the opinions of their authors and are not meant to represent the official position of the society.

First published in 1976 by David Philip, Publisher (Pty) Ltd, 3 Scott Road, Claremont, Cape Province, South Africa

First published in Great Britain in 1977 by Darton, Longman, and Todd Ltd, 85 Gloucester Road, London SW7 4SU

U.S. edition published in 1978 by Orbis Books, Maryknoll, New York 10545

Revised edition published in 1992 by Orbis Books, Maryknoll, New York 10545, and Darton, Longman, and Todd Ltd, 85 Gloucester Road, London SW7 4SU

**Library of Congress Cataloging-in-Publication Data**

Nolan, Albert, 1934-
   Jesus before Christianity / Albert Nolan. — Rev. ed.
  p.  cm.
   Includes bibliographical references and index.
   ISBN 0-88344-832-7
   1. Jesus Christ — Person and offices.  I. Title.
BT202.N64    1992
232 — dc20                    92-5604
                                     CIP

To the People of the Third World

# CONTENTS

## PART FOUR
## CONFRONTATION

# PREFACE TO THE THIRD EDITION 1992

All the changes that have been made in this third edition are concerned with the sexist language and assumptions of the original, which was first published some fifteen years ago. The number of changes required to make the language and the assumptions inclusive has astounded me. I could not have done it alone even if I had had plenty of time. My colleague and friend, Denise Ackerman, spent many precious hours pouring over the text and providing me with minute and invaluable advice. In the end the decisions about how to make the adjustments were left to me and I alone take responsibility for them, but the real hard work was done by Denise, and I am truly grateful to her for that.

Among other things, I had to decide what to do with well-known terms like "kingdom of God" and "son of man." Alternatives need to be developed and are being developed. In the meantime it is important to ensure that the reader knows what we are referring to. We are referring to what has generally and unfortunately been called the "kingdom of God" and the "son of man." But it is equally important to indicate that these well-known terms are sexist. This I have chosen to do by making use of quotation marks.

Another decision concerned the scribes and the Pharisees, Sadducees, Essenes, and Zealots. They cannot be referred to as men and women of religion because they excluded women from their ranks. I have therefore spoken about them in the masculine form as men of religion.

One of the really great signs of hope in the world today is the way in which women are claiming their rights and opening the eyes of men to the injustice of patriarchy in all its forms. How grateful we ought to be to God for this grace of our times.

In other ways, too, our times are changing. Although the description of the "present historical situation" in chapter one is now somewhat dated, nevertheless the crisis remains and if anything it is more serious than it was fifteen years ago. Consequently the perspective on Jesus proposed in chapter one remains as valid as ever.

ALBERT NOLAN

# ACKNOWLEDGMENTS

I am indebted to very many friends for suggestions and criticisms and to very many scholars for the fruits of their research. But I would like to acknowledge here my special indebtedness to J. Jeremias, L. Gaston, E. Trocmé, G. von Rad, J. D. M. Derrett and G. Vermes, whose works opened my eyes to things which I would certainly not otherwise have seen.

All translations of the biblical texts have been taken from the Jerusalem Bible (JB) except where otherwise indicated. AV = Authorized Version, RV = Revised Version, RSV = Revised Standard Version, NEB = New English Bible, and an asterisk (*) indicates that I have made my own translation of the text. The abbreviation par (or parr) after a biblical reference denotes "and the parallel text (or texts)."

Excerpts from *The Jerusalem Bible* copyright 1966 by Darton, Longman and Todd, Ltd and Doubleday & Company, Inc. used by permission of the publisher.

ALBERT NOLAN

# INTRODUCTION

The primary purpose of this book is neither faith nor history. It can be read and is designed to be read without faith. Nothing about Jesus will be presupposed or assumed. The reader is invited to take a serious and honest look at a man who lived in first-century Palestine and to try to see him through the eyes of his contemporaries. My interest is in the man as he was before he became the object of Christian faith.

Faith in Jesus is not our starting-point, but it will be, I hope, our conclusion. However, this does not mean that the book was written for the apologetic purpose of defending the Christian faith. No attempt has been made to *save* Jesus or the Christian faith. Jesus does not need me or anyone else to save him. He can look after himself, because the truth can look after itself. If our search for the truth leads us to faith in Jesus, then it will not be because we have tried to save this faith at all costs, but because we have rediscovered it as the only way in which *we* can be "saved" or liberated. Only the truth can make us free (Jn 8: 32).

We will be searching for the historical truth about Jesus, but even this is not our primary purpose. The method is historical, but the purpose is not. Despite the consistent use of strict historical criticism and methods of research, our interest is not the academic pursuit of history for the sake of history.

This book has an urgent and practical purpose. I am concerned about people, the daily sufferings of so many millions of people, and the prospect of much greater suffering in the near future. My purpose is to find out what can be done about it.

1

# PART ONE

# CATASTROPHE

## Chapter 1

# A NEW PERSPECTIVE

Many millions throughout the ages have venerated the name of Jesus, but few have understood him and fewer still have tried to put into practice what he wanted to see done. His words have been twisted and turned to mean everything, anything and nothing. His name has been used and abused to justify crimes, to frighten children and to inspire men and women to heroic foolishness. Jesus has been more frequently honored and worshipped for what he did not mean than for what he did mean. The supreme irony is that some of the things he opposed most strongly in the world of his time were resurrected, preached and spread more widely throughout the world—in his name.

Jesus cannot be fully identified with that great religious phenomenon of the Western world known as Christianity. He was much more than the founder of one of the world's great religions. He stands above Christianity as the judge of all it has done in his name. Nor can historical Christianity claim him as its exclusive possession. Jesus belongs to all humanity.

Does this mean that all human beings (Christian or non-Christian) are free to interpret Jesus in their own way, to shape Jesus according to their own likes and dislikes? It is very easy to use Jesus for one's own purposes—good or bad. But he was an historical person who had some very strong convictions himself—he was willing to die for them. Is there no way in which all of us (with or without faith) can give Jesus the chance, once again today, to speak for himself?

It is clear that we would have to begin by putting aside all our preconceived ideas about him. We cannot begin by assuming that he is divine or that he is the Messiah or the Savior of the world. We cannot even begin with the assumption that he was a good and honest man. Nor can we begin with the assumption that he was definitely *not* any of these things. We must put aside all our images of Jesus, conservative and progressive, devotional and academic, so that we may listen to him with an open mind.

It is possible to approach Jesus without any presuppositions *about him,* but it is not possible to approach him without any presuppositions at all. The complete open mind is a blank mind that can understand nothing at all. We must have some kind of position, some kind of vantage-point or perspective, if we are to see and understand anything. A work of art, for example, can be seen and appreciated without any presuppositions about what it is supposed to be, but it cannot be seen at all except from a vantagepoint. It can be viewed from this or that angle, but it cannot be observed from no angle at all. The same is true of history. We cannot obtain a view of the past except from the place where we are standing at the moment. "Historical objectivity is not a reconstruction of the past in its unrepeatable factuality, it is the truth of the past in the light of the present."[1] To imagine that one can have historical objectivity without a perspective is an illusion.

One perspective, however, can be better than another. The perspective of each successive age is not equally valuable and true. Just as the beauty of a work of art may be seen more clearly and strikingly from one angle than from another, so an event of the past may be seen more clearly and distinctly from the perspective of one age than another. Not that we have any choice in this matter. The only perspective open to us is the one given to us by the historical situation in which we find ourselves. If we cannot achieve an unobstructed view of Jesus from the vantagepoint of our present circumstances, then we cannot achieve an unobstructed view of him at all.

A modern perspective is not necessarily better than an older one. Nevertheless it sometimes happens that one's historical situation has striking similarities with a situation of the distant past. Then, despite the long interval of time, one is suddenly able to see that past situation with much greater clarity than any previous generation had been able to do. My contention will be that this is what has happened to us today with respect to Jesus of Nazareth.

This, of course, cannot be assumed; it will have to be discovered. Still less can we assume that Jesus has all the answers to *our* problems. There is no point in trying to *make* him relevant. All we can do is look at him from the perspective of our time with an open mind.

Our starting-point, then, is the urgent reality of our present historical situation.

Our age is characterized by problems that are a matter of life and death, not only for individuals, not only for whole nations, races and civilizations, but a matter of life and death for the entire human race. We are aware of problems that threaten the survival of humankind on this planet. Moreover, our age is further characterized by the fear that these problems may now be insoluble and that no one will be able to stop our headlong plunge toward the total destruction of the human species.

The first real awareness of this came with the bomb. Suddenly we found ourselves in a world capable of destroying itself—at the push of a button. We were all at the mercy of those persons at the other side of that button. Could they be trusted? The growing awareness of what was at stake made us feel more and more uneasy and insecure. The generation of young people who grew up during the late 1950s and early '60s with this as the only world they had ever known, were profoundly disorientated by it. Protest, pop, drugs, long hair and hippies were all symptoms of the unease generated by the bomb.

Today the fear of nuclear war seems to have abated. In part, this is due to the much publicized *détente* between the superpowers; but it is also true that people gradually develop an immunity to such frightening realities. Nevertheless we were not destined to be left in peace for long. Today we find ourselves faced with new threats, threats which, they say, will destroy us more certainly and inevitably than a nuclear war: the population explosion, the diminishing of our natural resources and food supplies, the pollution of our environment and the escalation of violence. Any one of these problems by itself would be threatening enough to our future; taken together they spell disaster.

There are various ways of trying to help people understand what the exponential growth of the earth's population really means. My imagination cannot cope with such large numbers, but when I am told that at present the world's population is increasing at the rate of over 80 million people a year, and I remember that, when I last looked it up, the population of Britain was about 50 million, I begin to appreciate what is happening. At the same time one hears various estimates of how much longer our supplies of coal, oil, petrol, natural gas and even fresh water will last. It seems that some of these natural resources will run out within my own lifetime. In the meantime the deserts are creeping up on us as soil erosion increases and more and more forests are destroyed. A single Sunday edition of the *New York Times* eats up 150 acres of forest land. And much more paper is used for toilet rolls than for writing or printing purposes.

Moreover, in recent years we have been made aware of the cumulative and far-reaching effects of pollution in rivers, seas and the very air we breathe. I have lived in cities where people are killed by the pollution in the air. The environmentalists say that if drastic changes are not introduced very soon, we shall all be killed by the by-products of our own progress.

There is no need to exaggerate these problems. Solutions can be found. But these solutions would require such radical and such dramatic changes in the values, concerns, thought-patterns and standards of living of so many people, especially in the dominant rich countries, that most observers regard them as virtually impossible. We *could* do something really drastic about conserving the earth's resources and searching for alternative sources of energy. But who would tolerate the consequent loss of profits and all the extra expense? We *could* ignore the extra cost of adopting methods of transport and production that do not pollute the earth. Those of us who have a high standard of living *could* reduce this voluntarily by giving up all non-essentials—including our excessive use of paper. A much lower standard of living need not mean a lower quality of life, in fact it might improve the quality of our lives. But where would we find the human or moral resources to motivate so many of us to make such fundamental changes?[2]

It seems difficult enough to persuade people to curtail their present excesses in order to secure their own future; it would be far more difficult to ask them to do so for the sake of others, and well-nigh impossible to persuade them to make all the necessary sacrifices for the sake of the billions who have not yet been born.

On the other hand it is equally true that the world abounds in women and men of goodwill who appreciate the problems, are deeply concerned and would do anything to help. But what *can* they do? What can any individual or any number of individuals actually do about it all? What we are up against is not people but the impersonal forces of a system which has its own momentum and its own dynamics.[3] How often one hears the cry of hopeless resignation, "You cannot fight the system."

This indeed is the heart of the problem. We have built up an all-inclusive political and economic system based upon certain assumptions and values and now we are beginning to realize that this system is not only counter-productive—it has brought us to the brink of disaster—but it has also become our master. Nobody seems to be able to change it or control it. The most frightening discovery of all is that there is *nobody at the helm* and that the impersonal machine that we have so carefully designed will drag us along inexorably to our destruction.[4]

The system was not designed to cope with a population explosion. There is, for example, no political machinery that would enable the people of an impossibly overcrowded nation like Bangladesh to settle in the vast unpopulated areas of another nation such as Australia. The system of "nationalized" politics renders any such solution unthinkable.

From an economic point of view, the system produces both wealth and poverty at the same time. The rich are getting richer and the poor poorer. The more the poor nations try to measure up to the standards of development and economic growth demanded by the system, the poorer and more underdeveloped they become. The system is competitive, but everyone does not in fact have an equal chance. The more you have, the more you can make, and the more you can make, the less there is for those who do not have enough to compete with you. It is a vicious circle in which the poor are always the losers. More than one billion people — about one in five of the world's entire population — experience hunger for at least part of every year as the agricultural seasons pass with their meager fruits. They also lack clean water, elementary education, and basic health care.[5] Hundreds of millions of people are born into this world to experience little more than the pangs of hunger and the sufferings which result from malnutrition and deprivation. Only God knows how many millions die of starvation. Our *present* situation has become too horrible to contemplate — let alone the future.

The system was not designed to solve such problems. It can produce more and more wealth, but it is incapable of ensuring that even the bare necessities of life are evenly distributed. This is because it is geared to profits rather than to people. People can only be taken into account in so far as their welfare produces greater profits. The system is a monster which devours people for the sake of its profits.

Worse still, it seems that the system is now pressing its demands and defending itself with more and more violence. Quite apart from the institutional violence of injustice, oppression and exploitation, we are now witnessing the multiplication of military governments throughout the world. One does not have to travel very widely in the Third World in order to understand why the system can be maintained only by a military dictatorship. Many of those who are trying to fight the system have resorted to violence or are threatening to do so. Institutional violence leads to revolutionary violence, which in turn leads to more institutional violence in the form of riot police, detention without trial, torture, military governments and political murders — which then leads to more revolutionary violence. If something really drastic cannot be done about all the other problems (population, poverty, pollution, wastage, inflation and diminishing resources), the system will lead us into a "spiral of violence," as Helder Camara[6] calls it, which will rapidly include us all in an act of mutual destruction.

There is no point in exaggerating these problems for ideological purposes and yet, on the other hand, we cannot afford to ignore them or argue them away. We are being fed on a daily diet of new insights into the magnitude, complexity and insolubility of our problems. This creates an image of the future which is more frightening than all the old images of hell. The fundamental reality of life today, on any reckoning, is the prospect of a veritable *hell on earth.*

Organized religion has been of very little help in this crisis. In fact it has sometimes tended to make matters worse. The type of religion that emphasizes a supernatural world *in such a way* that one does not need to be concerned about the future of this world and all its peoples, offers a form of escape that makes it all the more difficult to solve our problems.

The one salutary effect of this moment in our history, its one redeeming feature, is that it can force us to be honest. What is the use of keeping up the facade or trying to save face when everything threatens to collapse around us? In this moment of truth who wants to indulge in the ecclesiastical and academic quibbles of the past? The person who has faced the present world crisis becomes impatient with those who continue to get excited about trivial and irrelevant problems, those who seem to be fiddling while Rome burns. The prospect of an unparalleled catastrophe can have a very sobering effect upon us.

Now it so happens, as I hope to show, that Jesus of Nazareth faced basically the same problem — even if it was on a much smaller scale. He lived in an age when it seemed that the world was about to come to an end. Despite differences of opinion about how, why and when, very many Jews at that time were convinced that the world was on the brink of an apocalyptic catastrophe. It was in view of this catastrophe, as we shall see, and in terms of his own understanding of it, that Jesus set out on his mission. With what I would like to call an unparalleled leap of creative imagination, this man saw a way out, and indeed more than a way out — he saw the way to total liberation and fulfillment for humankind.

We are faced with the same terrifying prospects. This not only enables us to appreciate Jesus' concern about an impending disaster, it also makes his possible insights into what can be done about it of supreme relevance to us. And yet we dare not presume that he has all the answers and that we know what those answers are. Nor can we presume that his insights will be irrelevant and that we can safely ignore them. Our situation is so critical that we dare not leave any stone unturned in our search for a way out.

It is ironical that Jesus' concern about "the end of the world," which proved to be such a stumbling-block to previous generations of New Testament scholars, is today the very thing that makes him of particular interest to us. Our present historical circumstances have quite unexpectedly provided us with a new perspective on Jesus of Nazareth.

*Chapter 2*

# THE PROPHECY OF JOHN THE BAPTIST

The four small books that we call the gospels are not biographies and were never intended to be. Their purpose was to show how Jesus could be relevant to people who lived *outside* Palestine a generation or two *after* Jesus' death. This first generation of Christians obviously did not feel the need for an exact biography of Jesus' life. They wanted to know how Jesus might be relevant to them in their situation outside Palestine.

We today are no more in need of a biography than that first generation or any other generation of Christians. Like them we need a book about Jesus that will show us what he might mean to us today in our situation. An exact chronicle of names, places and dates seldom allows an historical figure to come to life again for a later generation.

However, we can enable Jesus to come to life again for us today only by going back behind the four gospels to discover for ourselves what Jesus had to offer to the people of Palestine in his time. We don't need a biography but we do need to know the historical truth about Jesus.

If we read carefully between the lines of the four gospels and if we make full use of the information available about the contemporary situation, we shall be able to uncover a great deal of historical information about Jesus.[1] This is possible because, although the gospels were written for a later generation, they make use of sources that go back to Jesus and his contemporaries. In many places it is even possible to capture the actual words used by Jesus and to retrace exactly what he did (his *ipsissima vox et facta*). But what is of far greater importance is to uncover Jesus' original intentions (his *ipsissima intentio*).[2] If our purpose is to discover what Jesus was trying to achieve in his time, then it will sometimes be more valuable to know how his contemporaries lived and thought, and how they must have reacted to him, than to know exactly what words he used or what form his deeds took. Knowing these words and these deeds would be of value only in so far as they too might help us to uncover his original intentions.

What was Jesus trying to do? What did he hope to achieve for the people amongst whom he worked in first-century Palestine?

One of the best ways of uncovering Jesus' intentions would be to look for evidence of his decisions and choices. If we could find an historically certain incident in which Jesus made a choice between two or more alternatives, we should have a very important clue to the direction of his thinking. This we have at the beginning of all the gospels: Jesus chose to be baptized by John.

Whatever else Jesus' baptism might have meant, it implied a decision to align himself with John the Baptist rather than with any of the other voices or movements of the time. If we could understand how John the Baptist differed from his contemporaries, we should have our first clue to the direction of Jesus' thinking. We know enough about the history of the times to do this.

The Romans colonized Palestine in 63 B.C.E. In accordance with their policy of appointing native rulers in their colonies, they eventually made Herod, the most powerful claimant, king of the Jews. Jesus was born during the reign of this Herod, known as Herod the Great. In 4 B.C.E. (by modern calculation) Herod died and his kingdom was divided up amongst his three sons. Herod Archelaus was given Judaea and Samaria, and Herod Antipas Galilee and Peraea, while Herod Philip received the most northerly regions.

Archelaus, however, was unable to cope with the restless discontent of the people. The Romans became concerned. Eventually they deposed Archelaus and sent out a Roman procurator to govern Judaea and Samaria. Jesus was about 12 years old at the time. It was the beginning of direct Roman rule, the beginning of the last and most turbulent epoch in the history of the Jewish nation, the epoch that ended with the almost total destruction of the temple, the city and the nation in 70 C.E., and their final and complete destruction in 135 C.E., the epoch during which Jesus lived and died and during which the first communities of Christians had to find their feet.

The epoch began with a rebellion. The issue was taxation. The Romans had begun to take a census of the population and to draw up an inventory of the resources of the country, for the purpose of taxation. The Jews objected on religious grounds and rose up in rebellion. The leader of this rebellion was a man named Judas the Galilean, who founded a religiously inspired movement of freedom fighters.[3]

The Romans soon checked this first uprising and then as a warning crucified no fewer than two thousand of the rebels. But the movement continued. The Jews called them Zealots; the Romans called them bandits. They were of course an underground movement, no doubt loosely organized, sometimes breaking up into factions and sometimes joining up with some newly formed group like the Sicarii, who specialized in assassinations.[4] Perhaps some joined in because they liked to fight but others were in deadly religious earnest, with the constant threat of torture and crucifixion hanging over their heads. For sixty years they continued to harass the Roman army of occupation with sporadic uprisings and occasional guerilla warfare. They developed from a group of rebels into a revolutionary army. Then, in 66 C.E., about thirty years after Jesus' death, with mounting popular support, they overthrew the Romans and took over the government of the country. But four years later a very powerful army was sent out from Rome to destroy them. It was a merciless massacre. The last group held out against the Romans from their mountain fortress of Masada until 73 C.E., when nearly a thousand of them chose to commit suicide rather than submit to Rome.

It must be emphasized that the Zealot movement was essentially religious in inspiration and purpose. At that time most of the Jews in Palestine believed that Israel was a theocracy, that is to say, they believed that they were God's chosen nation, that God was King, their only Lord and Master and that their land and resources belonged to God alone. To have accepted the Romans as their masters would have been an act of unfaithfulness to God. To have paid taxes to Caesar would have been to give to Caesar what belonged to God. The Zealots were faithful Jews, zealous for the law and for the sovereignty and kingship of God.

The Pharisees would have had no quarrel with the Zealots on this score.[5] Six thousand Pharisees refused to sign the oath of allegiance to Caesar, and the Romans had to waive this requirement for their Jewish subjects.[6] But most of the Pharisees did not feel impelled to take up arms against the Romans, presumably because the odds were so heavily loaded against them. Their principal concern was the reform of Israel itself. God had abandoned them to the Roman yoke because of Israel's unfaithfulness to the law and the traditions of the fathers.

The Pharisees paid their taxes to Rome under protest but then separated themselves off from everyone who was not faithful to the law and the traditions, in order to form closed communities, the faithful remnant of Israel. Their name means "the separate ones," i.e., the holy ones, the true community of Israel.[7] Their morality was legalistic and bourgeois, a matter of reward and punishment. God loved and rewarded those who kept the law and hated and punished those who did not. The Pharisees believed in an after-life, in the resurrection of the dead and in a future Messiah whom God would send to liberate them from the Romans.

The Essenes went very much further than the Pharisees in their striving for perfection. Many of them separated themselves completely from society and went to live a celibate and ascetic life in camps in the desert. They were even more concerned than the Pharisees about ritual impurity and contamination by the wicked and unclean world. They observed daily and meticulously the rites of purification originally prescribed for priests who were about to offer sacrifice in the Temple.

The Essenes rejected everyone who did not belong to their "sect." The priestly regime in the Temple was regarded as corrupt. All outsiders were to be hated as the "sons of darkness."

Love and respect were reserved for the members of their group—the "sons of light." They alone were the faithful remnant of Israel.

Their strict separation and rigorous discipline must be understood as their response to the belief that the end of the world was near. They were preparing for the coming of the Messiah (or perhaps two Messiahs) and for the great war in which they as the "sons of light" would destroy the "sons of darkness," the armies of Satan. The first of the "sons of darkness" to be destroyed would be the Romans.[8]

The Essenes were therefore just as warlike as the Zealots[9] but for them the time was not yet ripe. They were waiting for the day of the Lord. Around 66 C.E., when the Zealots began to overpower the Romans, the Essenes seem to have joined in, only to be eventually destroyed together with the Zealots and others.[10]

In the midst of these outbursts of exceptional religious fervor, the Sadducees were the conservatives. They clung to the most ancient Hebrew traditions and rejected all novelties of belief and ritual.[11] The after-life and the resurrection of the dead were regarded as novelties. Rewards and punishments were to be found in this life. The Sadducees were therefore expedient. They collaborated with the Romans and endeavored to maintain the *status quo.*

The Sadducees were to a very large extent, though not exclusively, members of the wealthy aristocracy: the chief priests and elders.[12] The chief priests were a special class of priests. They not only offered sacrifices like other priests, they were also responsible for the organization and administration of the Temple. The priesthood was of course hereditary.

The elders were the lay nobility, the old aristocratic families who owned most of the land.[13]

The Sadducee party would also have included some scribes or rabbis although most of these were Pharisees. The scribes or rabbis were the men of learning. They were at the same time theologians, lawyers and teachers but they were not priests.

Thus in the gospels the Sadducees are frequently referred to as "the chief priests, elders and scribes" or as "the leaders of the people." They were the ruling, upper class.

Mention should also be made of a small group of anonymous writers who indulged in a type of literature which we today call *apocalyptic*. They were seers or visionaries who believed that the secrets of God's plan for history and especially for the end of the world had been indirectly revealed to them. As they saw it, God had predetermined all times and epochs, revealing secret plans to the men of ancient times like Enoch, Noah, Esdras, Abraham and Moses. The apocalyptic writers had now come to know these secrets and they were recording them on behalf of the ancients for the sake of the learned men of their own time.[14]

These writers were possibly scribes and they may have belonged to the Pharisee or Essene parties but we cannot be sure of that. They were anonymous and remain anonymous to this day.

In the midst of all these religio-political movements and speculations there was one man who stood out as a sign of contradiction. John the Baptist was different precisely because he was a prophet, and indeed, like so many of his predecessors of old, a prophet of doom and destruction. Superficial similarities with the Essenes or the apocalyptic writers or anyone else should never blind us to the fact that John was as different from his contemporaries as any prophet ever was. While others looked forward to the "age to come" when the faithful of Israel would triumph over their enemies, John prophesied doom and destruction for Israel.[15]

There had been no prophet in Israel for a very long time. Everyone was painfully aware of this, as all the literature of the period attests.[16] The spirit of prophecy had been quenched. God was silent. All one could hear was "the echo of his voice." It was even felt that certain decisions would have to be postponed "until a trustworthy prophet should arise" (1 Mc 14:41; see also 4:45–46).

This silence was broken by the voice of John the Baptist in the wilderness. His style of life, his way of speaking and his message were a conscious revival of the tradition of the prophets. The evidence we have about him, both within the New Testament and outside of it, is unanimous on this point.

John's prophetic message was a simple one. God was angry with the people and planned to punish them. God was about to intervene in history to condemn and destroy Israel. John pictured this destruction as a great forest fire before which the vipers flee (Mt 3:8 par), in which trees and chaff are burnt (Mt 3:10, 12 par), and in which people will be engulfed as in a baptism of fire (Mt 3:11 par). He also made use of the metaphors of the axe and the winnowing-fan. These are the metaphors of the prophets. They have nothing in common with the wild images of the apocalyptic writers.[17] There is no reason to believe that John was referring to hell in the after-life or to a cosmic upheaval. The forest fire is an image of hell on earth.

God's fiery judgment upon Israel would be executed, according to John, by a human being. John spoke of him as "the one who is to come" (Mt 3:11 parr; Mt 11:3 par). He is even now standing ready with his axe or his winnowing-fan. *"He* will baptize you with . . . fire" (Mt 3:11 par).

A prophecy is not a prediction, it is a warning or a promise. The prophet warns Israel about God's judgment and promises God's salvation. Both the warning and the promise are conditional. They depend upon the free response of the people of Israel. If Israel does not change, the consequences will be disastrous. If Israel does change, there will be an abundance of blessings. The practical purpose of a prophecy is to persuade the people to change or repent. Every prophet appealed for a conversion.

Unlike his contemporaries who were not prophets, John addresses his warning and his appeal to all Israel. They must not imagine that it is the Gentiles who are heading for destruction and that the children of Abraham will be spared because of their ancestry and race. "Do not presume to tell yourselves, 'We have Abraham for our father,' because, I tell you, God can raise children for Abraham from these stones" (Mt 3:9). God can destroy Israel and create a new people (children of Abraham) if Israel does not repent.

John appealed to sinners, prostitutes, tax collectors and soldiers as well as scribes and Pharisees (Lk 3:12, 14; Mt 21:32). He even challenged the Jewish king or tetrarch, Herod Antipas (Mk 6:18 par; Lk 3:19). There is no question here of gathering together a remnant or founding a "sect."[18] Everyone must change.

The earlier prophets had expected Israel to change as a whole in the person of its king or leading men. John, like the later prophets, expected each individual in Israel to repent and experience a personal change of heart. This is surely the fundamental meaning of John's practice of baptism. It does not matter what precedents there might be for the rite itself. What matters is the use that John made of it. John's baptism was a sign of individual and personal repentance. "They confessed their sins" and were then baptized (Mk 1:5 par).

This baptism is said to have been for or toward (*eis*) the forgiveness of sins (Mk 1:4 parr). In the context, the forgiveness of sins would mean being spared from the future punishment.[19] If the whole of Israel or perhaps the majority of the children of Abraham were to repent, God would cease to be angry and relent, so that the catastrophe would not take place at all. It is not clear whether, if the catastrophe did take place, those who had been baptized would be spared as individuals or not. Everything depends upon what kind of catastrophe John had in mind. Was it a war? More often than not the disaster which the prophets had in mind was a war in which Israel was defeated.[20] The innocent are seldom spared in a war. But there is not enough evidence for us to decide what John had in mind or whether he had thought about it at all.

It is also significant that the kind of change for which John appealed had nothing to do with ritual purity or petty details of sabbath observance; nor had it anything to do with not paying taxes to Gentiles. John appealed for what we would call social morality.

> If anyone has two tunics he must share with the man who has none, and the one with something to eat must do the same . . .
>
> To the tax collectors he said, "Exact no more than your rate!" . . .
>
> To the soldiers he said, "No intimidation! No extortion! Be content with your pay!" (Lk 3:11–14)

Herod he criticized for divorcing his wife to marry the wife of his half-brother (another Herod) and for all his other crimes

(Lk 3:19). But Josephus, the contemporary Jewish historian, maintains that Herod arrested John for political reasons.[21] He was afraid that John would turn the people against him. Herod could not afford to lose the support of his people especially in view of the political consequences of his re-marriage. In order to marry Herodias he had divorced the daughter of Aretas II, the ruler of the nearby kingdom of the Nabataeans. This would be viewed not only as a personal insult but also as a breach of a political alliance.[22] The Nabataeans were therefore preparing for war. As far as Herod was concerned John was only making matters worse for him by criticizing his divorce and re-marriage and by prophesying divine retribution. Some years later the Nabataeans attacked and defeated Herod, who had to call in the Romans to rescue him and his kingdom.

John was arrested and beheaded because he dared to speak out against Herod too.

John the Baptist was the only person in that society who impressed Jesus. Here was the voice of God warning the people of an impending disaster and calling for a change of heart in each and every individual. Jesus believed this and joined in with those who were determined to do something about it. He was baptized by John.

Jesus may not have agreed with John in every detail. Later, as we shall see, he certainly came to differ somewhat from John. But the very fact of his baptism by John is conclusive proof of his acceptance of John's basic prophecy: Israel is heading for an unprecedented catastrophe. And in choosing to believe this prophecy, Jesus immediately shows himself to be in basic disagreement with all those who reject John and his baptism: the Zealots, Pharisees Essenes, Sadducees, scribes and apocalyptic writers. None of these groups would have been willing to believe a prophet who, like the prophets of old, prophesied against all Israel.

Jesus' point of departure, then, was the impending judgment of Israel, an unprecedented catastrophe. There is plenty of evidence to show that Jesus repeated this prophecy again and again throughout his life. In fact in several of the texts which have come down to us, Jesus is far more explicit than John about

what the impending disaster would entail. We quote a few of
them:

A time is coming when your enemies will raise fortifica-
tions all around you, when they will encircle you and hem
you in on every side; they will dash you and the children
inside your walls to the ground; they will leave not one
stone standing on another within you — and all because you
did not recognize your opportunity when God offered it!
(Lk 19:43–44)

When you see Jerusalem surrounded by armies, you must
realize that she will soon be laid desolate. Then those in
Judaea must escape to the mountains, those inside the city
must leave it . . . For this is the time of vengeance . . . Alas
for those with child, or with babies at the breast, when
those days come. For great misery will descend on the land
and wrath on this people. (Lk 21:20–23)

But Jesus said, "Daughters of Jerusalem, do not weep for
me; weep rather for yourselves and for your children." (Lk
23:28)

People told him about the Galileans whose blood Pilate
had mingled with that of their sacrifices . . . He said, ". . .
unless you repent you will all be destroyed as they were."
(Lk 13:1, 3*)

There can be no doubt about what is being referred to here:
the destruction of Jerusalem in a war with the Romans. In true
prophetic style Jesus prophesies an unparalleled military defeat
for Israel. The divine judgment would be a terrible massacre,
and the executors of the judgment would be the Romans. Only
those who have the sense to flee will be spared (Mk 13:14–20
parr). This is precisely what did happen in 70 C.E.

Most scholars have not given much attention to these and
similar texts (Mk 13:2; 23:37–39 = Lk 13:34–35; Lk 11:49–51;
17:26–37). They are quite commonly dismissed as predictions
inserted into the text after the event (*vaticinia ex eventu*). But

recent scholarly research has shown quite conclusively that this is not so.

It was C. H. Dodd[23] who first showed that these passages could not have been written after the event because they are modelled on the scriptural references to the first fall of Jerusalem in 586 B.C.E. and they make no allusion to the distinctive features of the fall in 70 C.E. Lloyd Gaston comes to much the same conclusions. He spent ten years in research on this question and produced a voluminous scholarly work which is very convincing indeed, although little known and seldom read.[24]

There can be no doubt that Jesus did prophesy the destruction of Jerusalem by the Romans. The early Christians may have touched up his words a little but even this must have been done before the events of 70 C.E. It was John the Baptist who first foresaw the disaster, although we do not know what exactly he envisaged. Jesus agreed with John and reading the signs of the times saw quite clearly that Israel was on a collision course with Rome. Both Jesus and John, like the prophets of the Old Testament, expressed this imminent disaster in terms of a divine judgment.

The very thought of it made Jesus weep (Lk 19:41) as it had made the prophet Jeremiah weep centuries before. But what was he to do about it?

# PART TWO

# PRAXIS

## Chapter 3

# THE POOR AND THE OPPRESSED

Jesus may have begun by following John's example and baptizing people in the Jordan (Jn 3:22–26). If so, he soon gave up this practice (Jn 4:1–3). There is no evidence whatsoever that, after he left the Jordan and the desert, he ever baptized anyone or sent anyone to be baptized by John or by anyone else. Many people thought of him as John the Baptist's successor, but, successor or not, Jesus did not baptize. Instead he went to seek out, help and serve the lost sheep of the house of Israel.

Here we have a second decision, a second indisputable clue to the mind and intentions of Jesus. He did not feel called to save Israel by bringing everyone to a baptism of repentance in the Jordan. He decided that something else was necessary, something which had to do with the poor, the sinners and the sick—the lost sheep of the house of Israel.

The people to whom Jesus turned his attention are referred to in the gospels by a variety of terms: the poor, the blind, the lame, the crippled, the lepers, the hungry, the miserable (those who weep), sinners, prostitutes, tax collectors, demoniacs (those possessed by unclean spirits), the persecuted, the downtrodden, the captives, all who labor and are overburdened, the rabble who know nothing of the law, the crowds, the little ones, the least, the last and the babes or the lost sheep of the house of Israel.[1] The reference here is to a well-defined and unmistakable section of the population. Jesus generally refers to them as the poor or the little ones; the Pharisees refer to the same people as sinners or the rabble who know nothing of the law.[2] Today some might refer to this section of the population as the lower classes; others would call them the oppressed.

So much has been written about the historical circumstances in which Jesus lived and about all the "important" events which led up to the religious and political situation of the time. But this, like most historical writing, tells us only what the "important" people were doing and saying: the kings and princes, the powerful and the wealthy, the oppressors and their armies. The true history of humankind is the history of suffering[3] — something about which one finds precious little in history books. What about all those who suffered on account of the glorious battles of history? What about the daily sufferings of those who were oppressed when this or that king began his glorious reign? It may be possible to understand Napoleon without understanding the history of suffering in his time but it is certainly not possible to understand Jesus except against this kind of background. We must therefore try to enter into the world of the poor and the oppressed as it was in first-century Palestine.

Although the term "poor" in the gospels does not refer exclusively to those who were economically deprived, it does include them. The poor were in the very first place the beggars. They were the sick and disabled who had resorted to begging because they were unemployable and without a relative who could afford to or was willing to support them. There were of course no hospitals, welfare institutions or disability grants. They were expected to beg for their bread. Thus, the blind, the deaf and dumb, the lame, the cripples and the lepers were generally beggars.

Then there were the widows and orphans: the women and children who had no one to provide for them and, in that society, no way of earning a living. They would have been dependent upon the almsgiving of pious societies and the Temple treasury.

Among the economically poor one should also include the unskilled day-laborers who were often without work, the peasants who worked on the farms and perhaps the slaves.

On the whole, the suffering of the poor was not destitution and starvation except during a war or a famine. They were sometimes hungry and thirsty, but, unlike millions today, they seldom starved. The principal suffering of the poor, then as now, was shame and disgrace. As the steward in the parable says, "I would be too ashamed to beg" (Lk 16:3).

The economically poor were totally dependent upon the "charity" of others. For the Oriental, even more so than for the Westerner, this is terribly humiliating. In the Middle East, prestige and honor are more important than food or life itself.[4] Money, power and learning give people prestige and status because they make them relatively independent and enable them to do things for others.[5] The really poor who are dependent upon others and have no dependents are at the bottom of the social ladder. They have no prestige and no honor. They are hardly human. Their lives are meaningless. A Westerner today would experience this as a loss of human dignity.

This is why the word "poor" can be extended to cover all the oppressed, all those who are dependent upon the mercy of others. And this too is why the word can even be extended to all those who rely entirely upon the mercy of God—the poor in spirit (Mt 5:3).[6]

The "sinners" were social outcasts. Anyone who for any reason deviated from the law and the traditional customs of the middle class (the educated and the virtuous, the scribes and the Pharisees) was treated as inferior, as low class. The sinners were a well-defined social class, the same social class as the poor in the broader sense of the word.

They would have included those who had sinful or unclean professions: prostitutes, tax collectors (publicans),[7] robbers, herdsmen, usurers and gamblers. Tax collectors were thought to be deceivers and thieves because their profession gave them the right to decide how much tax or toll had to be paid, and the right to include some commission for themselves. Many of them were no doubt dishonest. Similarly, herdsmen were suspected of leading their herds onto other people's land and pilfering the produce of the herd, which was also no doubt often true. These and other professions therefore carried with them a social stigma.

The sinners would also have included those who did not pay their tithes (one-tenth of their income) to the priests, and those who were negligent about the sabbath rest and about ritual cleanliness. The laws and customs on these matters were so complicated that the uneducated were quite incapable of understanding what was expected of them. Education in those days was a matter of knowing the scriptures. The scriptures were the law and the prophets, and the prophets were understood to be the ancient commentators upon the law. Education was therefore a matter of knowing the law and all its ramifications. The illiterate and uneducated were inevitably lawless and immoral. The *'am ha-arez,* or uneducated peasants, "the rabble who know nothing of the law" (Jn 7:49) were regarded by even the most enlightened Pharisees, like Hillel, as incapable of virtue and piety.[8]

There was no practical way out for the sinner. Theoretically the prostitute could be made clean again by an elaborate process of repentance, purification and atonement. But this would cost money, and her ill-gotten gains could not be used for the purpose. Her money was tainted and unclean. The tax collector would be expected to give up his profession and then make restitution plus one-fifth to everyone he had wronged. The uneducated would have to go through a long process of education before one could be sure that they were "clean." To be a sinner was therefore one's lot. One had been predestined to inferiority by fate[9] or the will of God. In this sense the sinners were captives or prisoners.

Their suffering therefore took the form of frustration, guilt and anxiety. They were frustrated because they knew that they would never be accepted into the company of "respectable" people. What they felt they needed most of all was prestige and public esteem,[10] and this is what was denied them. They did not even have the consolation of feeling that they were in God's good books. The educated people told them that they were displeasing to God and "they ought to know." The result was a neurotic or near-neurotic guilt complex which led inevitably to fear and anxiety about the many kinds of divine punishment that might befall them.

The poor and the oppressed have always been especially prone to disease. This was particularly true in the time of Jesus, not only because of the physical conditions in which they lived, but also and more significantly because of the psychological conditions. Very many of them seem to have suffered from mental illnesses, which in turn gave rise to psychosomatic conditions like paralysis and speech impediments. But here we must abandon our modern psychological point of view and try to enter into the world of sickness and disease as the people of Jesus' time understood them.

For the Jewish and pagan Oriental the body is the abode of a spirit.[11] God breathes a spirit into a person to make him or her live. At death this spirit leaves the body. During a lifetime other spirits could also inhabit a person's body—either a good spirit (the Spirit of God) or an evil, unclean spirit, a demon. This condition would be observable in the person's behavior. Whenever people were not themselves, when they were beside themselves and appeared to have lost control of themselves, then it was regarded as quite obvious that something had got into them. We still ask the question in English today, "What has got into her or him?"

As the Oriental would see it, it is not the person's own spirit that is now operating. Such a person is obviously possessed by some other spirit. Depending on how you evaluate his or her unusual behavior, you would call it a good or an evil spirit. Thus the extraordinary behavior and unusual flashes of insight on the part of a prophet (especially if he or she went into a trance) would be conceptualized as possession by the Spirit of God; whereas the pathological behavior of the mentally ill would be conceptualized as possession by an evil spirit.[12]

The symptoms manifested by the demoniac boy in the gospels are the symptoms of what we would call epilepsy: throwing himself on the ground or into the fire with temporary deafness, dumbness, convulsions, writhing and foaming at the mouth (Mk 9:17–27 parr). It is not difficult to understand how he could be thought of as being in the grip of some evil spirit. Perhaps the man with the unclean spirit who was thrown into convulsions in the synagogue (Mk 1:23–26 par) was also an epileptic. The Gerasene demoniac who lived among the tombs with the spirits of the dead was clearly a raving lunatic. "No one could secure him any more, even with a chain ... He snapped the chains and broke the fetters, and no one had the strength to control him.

All night and all day . . . he would howl and gash himself with stones" (Mk 5:3–5). He was obviously possessed by an unclean or evil spirit (Mk 5:2).

Some physical and psychosomatic illnesses were also thought of as the work of an evil spirit. Luke tells us of a weak and crippled woman who was "possessed by a spirit of weakness," that is to say, a spirit that enfeebled her body. "She was bent double" and is therefore described as having been "bound by Satan," that is to say, held in that position by the evil spirit dwelling in her (Lk 13:10–17). There are also spirits of deafness and dumbness who close the ears of the deaf and tie the tongues of the dumb (Mk 9:18, 25; 7:35). The high fever or delirium of Simon's mother-in-law is not explicitly called an evil spirit but it is personified in much the same way: "Jesus rebuked the fever and it left her" (Lk 4:39). The paralytic who had his sins forgiven (Mk 2:1–12 par) would appear to have been suffering from the psychosomatic effects of a severe guilt complex. He too might have been described as having a spirit of lameness although the gospels do not actually use that description.

It will be noticed that all these illnesses are what we would call dysfunctional. Diseases which appear outwardly on the skin would not have been described in this manner. They were defects of the body rather than of the spirit inhabiting the body. People who had any kind of disease which made them outwardly unclean were known as lepers. In ancient times leprosy was a generic term covering all skin diseases including sores and rashes. Lepers were not possessed by unclean spirits; nevertheless their bodily uncleanness was also the result of sin.[13]

All misfortunes, sicknesses and other disorders were evil. They were afflictions sent by God as punishments for sin—one's own sin or the sin of someone in one's household or the sins of one's ancestors. "Who sinned, this man or his parents, for him to have been born blind?" (Jn 9:2, see also Lk 13:2, 4). However, they did not suppose that God administered such punishments directly, but handed one over to the powers of evil (Job 1:12).

There was an original and basic truth—in this link between sin and suffering—to sin is to do something harmful to yourself or others. But the link had been thoroughly misconceived. They had been taught to think of sin as the failure to observe laws of which they were usually quite ignorant. Sin was therefore not always a fully deliberate act. One could sin by mistake or in ignorance. Similarly one might have to bear the guilt of someone else's sin. The children of any illegitimate sexual union and their children for ten generations were regarded as sinners.[14] Jews who were not racially pure or who could not trace their ancestry back far enough to prove their racial purity had to bear the social stigma of their ancestors who had sinned by mixing Jewish and pagan blood.[15] When sin was so mechanically imputed, its link with punishment and suffering had to be thought of in an equally mechanical manner.

We have here a fertile field for superstition, and many of the poor and uneducated were decidedly superstitious. Both the Jews and the Gentiles of Palestine made use of witchdoctors and sin diviners, who were thought to be able to divine the sinful source of any affliction.[16]

It was a dark and fearful world in which the helpless individual was threatened from all sides by hostile spirits and equally hostile people. They were at the mercy of evil spirits who might at any moment inflict them with sickness or madness; just as they were at the mercy of kings and tetrarchs who possessed them like property that could be acquired, used or disposed of as the politics of the moment required. They were often bled by taxation.

The poor and the oppressed were at the mercy of scribes who loaded legal burdens upon them and never lifted a finger to relieve them (Lk 11:46). They were denied civil rights. "No honorary offices could be conferred on them and they were not admitted as witnesses in trials."[17] "All the most important honors, positions of trust and public posts were reserved for full Israelites,"[18] that is to say, for those who were not sinners and who could prove that their ancestry was pure and legitimate. Sinners were excluded from the synagogue.

Such was the world of the "downtrodden," the "persecuted" and the "captives" (Lk 4:18; Mt 5:10). Today they would be called the oppressed, the *marginales* or the wretched of the earth—the people who don't count. But they were the overwhelming majority of the population in Palestine—the crowds or multitudes of the gospels. The middle class was very small and the upper classes even smaller.

Professional people, shopkeepers and tradesmen like carpenters and fishermen were "respectable" and middle class. The Pharisees, Essenes and Zealots were all educated men of the middle class. The Zealots may have included in their armies some of the rabble, who knew nothing of the law, especially toward the end in Jerusalem,[19] but on the whole the poor and the oppressed had no part in these religio-political movements.

The upper or ruling classes were enormously wealthy and lived in great luxury and splendor. Between the middle and the upper classes there was an immeasurable economic gap. The upper classes would include the royal household of the Herods, whose wealth was derived from taxation, the aristocratic priestly families (chief priests), who lived off the tithes and Temple tax, and the lay nobility (elders), who owned most of the land.[20]

Jesus came from the middle class. He was not by birth and upbringing one of the poor and the oppressed. It has often been pointed out that Jesus, unlike Paul, was not a Roman citizen and therefore did not have the rights of a Roman citizen. But within the society in which Jesus lived that was no real disadvantage. His only disadvantage, and that was a slight disadvantage applying only in Jerusalem, was that he was a Galilean. The orthodox Jews in Jerusalem tended to look down upon even middle-class Jews from Galilee.[21]

The remarkable thing about Jesus was that, although he came from the middle class and had no appreciable disadvantages himself, he mixed socially with the lowest of the low and identified himself with them. He became an outcast *by choice*.

Why did Jesus do this? What would make a middle-class man talk to beggars and mix socially with the poor? What would make a prophet associate with the rabble who know nothing of the law? The answer comes across very clearly in the gospels: compassion.

"He was moved with compassion for the crowds and he healed their sick" (Mt 14:14*). "He was moved with compassion because they were distressed and dejected like sheep without a shepherd" (Mt 9:36*, compare Mk 6:34). He was moved with compassion by the plight and the tears of the widow of Nain.

"Do not cry," he says to her (Lk 7:13). We are told explicitly that he had compassion on a leper (Mk 1:41), on two blind men (Mt 20:34) and on those who had nothing to eat (Mk 8:2 par).

Throughout the gospels, even when the word is not used, we can feel the movement of compassion. Over and over again Jesus says to people, "Don't cry," "Don't worry," "Don't be afraid" (e.g., Mk 5:36; 6:50; Mt 6:25–34; see also Mk 4:40; Lk 10:41). He was not moved by the grandeur of the great Temple buildings (Mk 13:1–2), he was moved by the poor widow who put her last cent into the Temple treasury (Mk 12:41–44). While everyone else was excited about the "miracle" of Jairus's daughter, he was concerned that she should be given something to eat (Mk 5:42–43).

What made the good Samaritan in the parable different was the compassion he felt for the man left half dead on the roadside (Lk 10:33). What made the loving father in the parable different was the excess of compassion he felt for his prodigal son (Lk 15:20). What made Jesus different was the unrestrained compassion he felt for the poor and the oppressed.

The English word "compassion" is far too weak to express the emotion that moved Jesus. The Greek verb *splagchnizomai* used in all these texts is derived from the noun *splagchnon,* which means intestines, bowels, entrails or heart, that is to say, the inward parts from which strong emotions seem to arise. The Greek verb therefore means a movement or impulse that wells up from one's very entrails, a gut reaction. That is why English translators have to resort to expressions like "he was *moved* with compassion or pity" (AV, RV, JB) or "he *felt* sorry" (JB) or "his *heart* went out to them" (NEB). But even these do not capture the deep physical and emotional flavor of the Greek word for compassion.

That Jesus was moved by some such emotion is beyond all reasonable doubt. It is an eminently human feeling which the evangelists and early Church would have had no apologetic reason for ascribing to Jesus. Besides, as we shall see, much of his activity and thinking and much of the impact he had upon people would remain unintelligible if he had not in fact been very deeply moved with compassion for the poor and the oppressed.

If the suffering of the poor and the oppressed had such a

powerful effect upon Jesus, what must the prospect of much greater suffering in the future have done to him? Compassion is a response to suffering. The thought of an imminent catastrophe, which would engulf so many in a blood-bath and produce sufferings too horrible to contemplate, must have shaken a man of such compassion and sensitivity. "Alas for those with child, or with babies at the breast, when those days come" (Lk 21:23). "They will dash to the ground you and your children" (Lk 19:44*).

Jesus, like Jeremiah, was moved to tears. But what could be done? It is all very well to feel compassionate and sympathetic but how could anyone do anything about it?

John relied upon a baptism of conversion; Jesus set out to liberate people from every form of suffering and anguish—present and future. How?

*Chapter 4*

# HEALING

There *were* doctors or physicians in those days. But they were few and far between, their knowledge of medicine was very limited, and the poor could seldom afford to consult them. We have already mentioned the use that was made of witchdoctors and sin diviners but there were also professional exorcists who claimed to be able to cast out evil spirits and who apparently sometimes succeeded in doing so.

The professional exorcists attributed their success to the precise observance of some ancient ritual formula. This ritual would have included incantations, symbolic actions, the use of certain substances and the invocation of the name of the ancient and wise man of God (like Solomon) to whom the ritual was supposed to have been revealed.[1] There is very little to distinguish this from magic.

However there was also the occasional, perhaps very occasional, holy man (like Hanina ben Dosa) who could produce rain or effect a cure by means of a simple and spontaneous prayer to God.[2]

Jesus was different from each and every one of these healers. Perhaps he did sometimes make use of his own saliva, a substance generally thought to be medicinal (Mk 7:33; 8:23). There was certainly a spontaneous concern to make some kind of physical contact with the sick person (e.g., Mk 1:31, 41; 6:56; 8:22–25). He touched them, took them by the hand or laid his hands on them. But he never made use of any kind of ritual formulae, incantations or invocations of names. It is very likely that he was accused of exorcising in the name of Beelzebub or Satan precisely because he had not invoked any other authority nor used any traditional ritual.[3]

There is a sense in which Jesus did indeed make use of spontaneous prayer (Mk 9:29) but his understanding of what was happening in such cases differs widely from that of the holy men who prayed for rain or cures. They relied upon their own holiness, their own esteem in the eyes of God;[4] Jesus relied upon the power of faith. It was not prayer as such that effected the cure, it was faith (Mt 21:22).

Over and again we are told that Jesus said to the person who had been cured, "Your faith has healed you."[5] This is a remarkable statement, which immediately lifts Jesus out of any of the contemporary categories of physician, exorcist, wonder-worker or holy man. He is saying in effect that it is not he who has healed the sick person, it is not by means of some psychic power that he has or by some special relationship with God. Nor is it to be attributed to the effectiveness of some magical formula, nor even to the simple medicinal properties of saliva. He is not even saying, at least not explicitly, that the person was healed by God.[6] *"Your faith* has healed you."

This is a truly astonishing claim. Jesus, like any believing Jew, would have realized that "everything is possible for *God"* (Mk 10:27). But Jesus differed from his contemporaries in understanding this to mean that "everything is possible for *anyone who has faith"* (Mk 9:23). The person who has faith becomes like God—all-powerful. "If you have faith, as a grain of mustard seed, nothing would be impossible for you . . . you could say to this mountain, 'Move from here to there' and it would move" (Mt 17:20*).

The mustard seed and the moving of mountains are both metaphors. Faith, *like* a mustard seed, is an apparently small and insignificant thing that can achieve impossibly great things. What faith can achieve is *like* moving mountains or, as Luke would have it, *like* moving a mulberry tree (17:6). One suspects some early confusion of metaphors here. Nevertheless, the point is clear enough. Faith, for Jesus, is an almighty power, a power that can achieve the impossible.[7]

Where John had relied upon a baptism of conversion, Jesus relied upon faith. The only power that can heal and save the world, the only power that can do the impossible, is the power of faith. "Your faith has saved you."

This faith is obviously not the same as subscribing to a creed or a set of doctrines and dogmas. And yet it is a conviction, a very strong conviction. The sick person has faith when he or she becomes convinced that they can and will be cured. When this conviction is strong enough, the cure is effected; they can get up and walk. If a person speaks with sufficient conviction, "with no hesitation in his heart but believing that what he says will happen, it will be done for him" (Mk 11:23). And if you pray with the very real conviction that "you have it already, it will be yours" (Mk 11:24). But if you once doubt or hesitate, nothing will happen. This is illustrated by the story of Peter walking on the water. He doubted for a moment and just then he began to sink (Mt 14:28–31). When Jesus' disciples first tried to cast out evil spirits, they did not succeed because their conviction was still weak and hesitant, they had too little faith (Mt 17:19–20).

This does not mean that the power of faith is simply the power of a strong conviction or the psychosomatic influence of a powerful suggestion which effects a cure by means of what is called "overpowering therapy."[8] Faith is not any conviction at all—true or false, good, bad or indifferent. It is a particular kind of conviction and it receives its power from the kind of conviction that it is. Faith is a good and a true conviction. It is the conviction that something can and will happen because it is good and because it is true that goodness can and will triumph over evil. In other words it is the conviction that God is good to humanity and that God can and will triumph over all evil. The power of faith is the power of goodness and truth, which is the power of God.

The opposite of faith is therefore fatalism. Fatalism is not a peculiar philosophy of life which once existed in some remote corner of the world. Fatalism is the prevailing attitude of most people, most of the time. It finds expression in statements like "Nothing can be done about it." "You can't change the world."

"You must be practical and realistic." "There is no hope." "There is nothing new under the sun." "You must accept reality." These are the statements of people who do not really believe in the power of God, people who do not really hope for what God has promised.

It will be noticed that this kind of faith is very closely related to hope. In fact, faith in the biblical sense of the word is almost indistinguishable from hope (e.g., Heb 11:1; Rom 4:18–22).[9] The most that one could say would be that faith and hope are two different aspects of one and the same attitude of mind, just as unbelief and despair are two different aspects of fatalism.

We have seen something of the fatalism of the poor, the sinners and the sick in the time of Jesus. The success of his healing activity must be seen as the triumph of faith and hope over fatalism. The sick, who had become resigned to their sickness as their lot in life, were encouraged to believe that they could and would be cured. Jesus' own faith, his own unshakable convictions, awakened this faith in them. Faith was an attitude that people caught from Jesus through their contact with him, almost as if it were a kind of infection. It could not be taught, it could only be caught. And so they begin to look to him to increase their faith (Lk 17:5) or to help their unbelief (Mk 9:24). Jesus was the initiator of faith. But once it had been initiated it could spread from one person to another. The faith of one person could awaken faith in another. The disciples were sent out to awaken faith in others.

Wherever the general atmosphere of fatalism had been replaced by an atmosphere of faith, the impossible began to happen. In Nazareth, his home town, there was a general lack of faith and that was why no "marvelous" or outstanding cures took place there (Mk 6:5–6). But elsewhere in Galilee people were healed and cured, evil spirits were cast out and lepers were cleansed. The miracles of liberation had begun to take place.

But were they really and truly miracles?

Miracles are very often thought of, both by those who believe in them and by those who do not, as events, or purported events, that contradict the laws of nature and that therefore cannot be explained by science or reason. But this is not at all what the Bible means by a miracle, as any biblical scholar will tell you.[10]

"The laws of nature" is a modern scientific concept. The Bible knows nothing about nature, let alone the laws of nature. The world is God's creation and whatever happens in the world, ordinary or extraordinary, is part of God's providence. The Bible does not divide events into natural and supernatural. God is in one way or another behind all events.

A miracle in the Bible is an unusual event which has been understood as an unusual *act of God,* a mighty work. Certain acts of God are called miracles or wonders because of their ability to astonish and surprise us, their ability to make us marvel and wonder. Thus creation is a miracle, grace is a miracle, the growth of an enormous mustard tree from a tiny seed is a miracle, the liberation of the Israelites from Egypt was a miracle, the kingdom of God will be a miracle. The world is full of miracles for those who have eyes to see them. If we are no longer able to wonder and marvel except when the so-called laws of nature are broken, then we must be in a sorry state.

The laws of nature are the working hypotheses of science. They have an extremely important and practical value for us. But we must recognize them for what they are. They have constantly to be reviewed and revised in the light of new evidence. Much of what was regarded as a law of nature in the seventeenth century would not be regarded as such today. Any good scientist will tell you that even the latest scientific theories are not the last words about what is possible or impossible in life. Many of them will tell you today that even alleged miracles cannot be excluded *a priori.*[11] There is much more to this mysterious world of ours than any of us have ever been able to comprehend.

The laws of nature then are no criteria at all for deciding what is a miracle and what is not. Something may well contradict the laws of nature as they are known to us at any given time without being a miracle or act of God, e.g., acupuncture, extra–sensory perception, bending forks with one's mind, and the feats of Indian yogis. On the other hand something may be a miracle even if it can be explained by perfectly natural causes. For the Jews the greatest miracle in the Bible was the Exodus miracle, the crossing of the Reed Sea (not the Red Sea, which is a mistranslation; the Reed Sea is a marsh to the North of the Red Sea).[12] All serious scholars today would agree that this crossing and the subsequent drowning of the Egyptian army can be explained by the natural phenomena of tides and winds, which were indeed "providential" for the Israelites. Nevertheless this remains the greatest miracle in the Old Testament. The embellishments which were added to the story through centuries of re-telling were intended only to underline our need to marvel at what God had done for the people of Israel.

A miracle then is an act of God which in its power and unusualness causes us to wonder and marvel. As such it can be called, and in the Bible is often called, a sign—a sign of God's power and providence, of justice and mercy, of God's will to save and liberate.

How then is one to understand the gospel accounts of Jesus' miracles?

There is a well-founded theory that Mark became dissatisfied with the portrait of Jesus as a teacher which was current in the Church at the time.[13] Those who had not known Jesus during his lifetime came to know him principally through his sayings and parables. Mark wished to correct this one-sided picture. He must, therefore, it is argued, have made contact, directly or indirectly, with the simple, uneducated villagers who had known Jesus in Galilee. The story-tellers of Galilee who had possibly never become Christians remembered and recounted what had impressed the poor and the oppressed most of all—Jesus' miracles. Miracles make much more interesting stories than sermons or wise sayings or new and original religious ideas. They could be told over and over again around the fire at night and with a few embellishments they would never fail to keep an audience enthralled.

It would have been from such story-tellers that Mark obtained most of his accounts of Jesus' miracles. There must have been other stories too which came down to him from Peter or one of the other disciples. In all these cases Mark would not have exercised the critical judgment of a modern historian. He was faithful to his sources. Besides, miracles were a particularly easy and convenient way of convincing his readers. The language of miracle was a language that anyone in those days could understand and appreciate.[14] Matthew and Luke probably followed Mark, but John seems to have had his own source of "signs" or "works" performed by Jesus.

It is therefore very likely that the miracle-stories which have been handed down to us in the gospels include embellishments and exaggerations and that they also include accounts of events that were not originally miracles or extraordinary marvels (e.g., the walking on the waters, the multiplication of the loaves, the cursing of the fig tree and the changing of the water into wine). A critical study of the texts tends to confirm this.[15]

Nevertheless, after this has been taken into account, it appears as an indubitable historical fact that Jesus did perform miracles, and that he did exorcise and heal people in a quite extraordinary manner. But what is even more extraordinary is that, despite their own concern to find the miraculous wherever possible, the gospel-writers faithfully record Jesus' extreme reluctance to perform miracles.

The Pharisees were constantly demanding of him a "sign from heaven," and each time he refused to attempt anything of the kind (Mk 8:11–13 parr; see also Lk 11:16; Jn 2:18; 4:48; 6:30). What they were looking for was some kind of spectacular miracle which would authenticate his mission and prove conclusively that he was a prophet sent by God. How else could they know whether to believe him or not? But Jesus quite confidently declares that no such sign shall be given and moreover that the generation which demands a miraculous sign is a wicked and unfaithful generation (Lk 11:29 parr).

Nothing shows more clearly how different Jesus was from the men of his generation. He regarded any attempt to produce an authenticating miracle as a Satanic temptation. Hence the story of his temptation in the desert, when Satan is said to have tempted him to jump off the pinnacle of the Temple. Jesus rejects this as a sinful attempt to put God to the test (Lk 4:12 par). Almost any other religious man in those days would have found it well-nigh impossible to resist the temptation to justify himself by means of heavenly proofs and signs.

Anyone who thinks that Jesus' *motive* for performing miracles of healing was a desire to prove something, to prove that he was the Messiah or Son of God, has thoroughly misunderstood him. His one and only motive for healing people was compassion. His only desire was to liberate people from their suffering and their fatalistic resignation to suffering. He was deeply convinced that this could be done and the miraculous success of his efforts must be attributed to the power of his faith. Nor did he think that he had any monopoly over compassion, faith and miraculous cures. What he wanted to do most of all was to awaken the same compassion and the same faith in the people around him. That alone would enable the power of God to become operative and effective in their midst.

Consequently, although Jesus did not set out to prove anything, his miraculous success did show that God was at work liberating his people because of the faith that Jesus had engendered in them.

# Chapter 5

# FORGIVENESS

John the Baptist preached to sinners. Hanina ben Dosa exorcised evil spirits from them.[1] But Jesus identified with them. He went out of his way to mix socially with beggars, tax collectors and prostitutes.

In societies where there are barriers between classes, races or other status groups, the separation is maintained by means of a taboo on social mixing. You do not share a meal or a dinner party, you do not celebrate, or participate in entertainments, with people who belong to another social group. In the Middle East sharing a meal at table with someone is a particularly intimate form of association and friendship. They would never even out of politeness eat and drink with a person of a lower class or status or with any person of whom they disapproved.

The scandal Jesus caused in that society by mixing socially with sinners can hardly be imagined by most people in the modern world today. It meant that he accepted them and approved of them and that he actually wanted to be "a *friend* of tax collectors and sinners" (Mt 11:19). The effect upon the poor and the oppressed themselves was miraculous.

That Jesus did mix socially with sinners is an assured historical fact. It can be found in four independent gospel traditions and in all the literary forms of the gospels.[2] Such a scandalous practice could not possibly have been invented by his subsequent, more "respectable" followers. We might even wonder whether the gospels have not perhaps played down this aspect of his praxis. Nevertheless the evidence we do have shows clearly enough that Jesus had what is called "table-fellowship" with sinners.

> "This man," they said, "*entertains*³ sinners and *feasts* with them." (Lk 15:2*)

> When he was *reclining* [at dinner] in his house, a number of tax collectors and sinners were *reclining* with Jesus and his disciples; for there were many of them among his followers. (Mk 2:15,* compare Mt 9:10; Lk 5:29)

> And you say, "Look, a glutton and a drunkard, a friend of tax collectors and sinners." (Lk 7:34 = Mt 11:19)

Jesus entertained sinners in his house. We have been inclined to take too literally the statement that "the son of man has nowhere to lay his head" (Mt 8:20 = Lk 9:58). Jesus travelled around very much and had therefore to sleep on the side of the road or in the houses of friends, but he did have a home in Capernaum, possibly in a house he shared with Peter, Andrew and their families (Mk 1:21, 29, 35; 2:1–2; Mt 4:13). The reference to *his* house in Mk 2:15 could mean Levi's house as Luke took it to mean (5:29) but it has been plausibly argued that it was Jesus' house.⁴ Besides, it is difficult to understand how Jesus could have been accused of entertaining sinners (Lk 15:2) if he did not have some kind of a home in which to do so.

The fact that guests were invited and the fact that they reclined at table show that the meals referred to in the gospels were feasts or dinner parties. At ordinary family meals to which guests had not been invited people sat upright at table in much the same way as we do.⁵ One reclined only at a feast or dinner party. Feasts or dinner parties need not be thought of as very elaborate and expensive meals (Lk 10:38–42). The company and conversation mattered more than the food. Nevertheless these dinner parties were such a common feature of Jesus' life that he could be accused of being a drunkard and a glutton.

According to Luke, Jesus once told his middle-class host that he ought to invite "the poor, the crippled, the lame, the blind" instead of always inviting his "friends, brothers, relations or rich neighbors" (14:12–13). We can assume that Jesus practiced what he preached and therefore that it was his custom to entertain not only tax collectors and sinners but also beggars and tramps.

On the other hand, Jesus must also have invited Pharisees and other "respectable" people to dine with him. If they invited him to their houses (Lk 7:36; 11:37; 14:1) he must surely have reciprocated by sometimes inviting them to his house. But how would the Pharisees and beggars manage at the same table? Would the Pharisees not have been afraid to lose status by accepting invitations to such meals?

It is this that makes one wonder whether the parable of the invited guests (Lk 14:15–24) was not perhaps based upon actual events in the life of Jesus. Did the "respectable" guests begin to make excuses when invited to his table? Did he send out his disciples "into the streets and alleys of the town" in order to bring in "the poor, the crippled, the blind and the lame" and even "to the open roads and hedgerows to compel people to come in"?

The beggars were no doubt reluctant at first and the sinners would have thought twice before inviting Jesus to their houses. To overcome such ingrained social customs Jesus would sometimes have had to compel the beggars to come, and to invite himself to the houses of sinners. Luke has illustrated the latter in his story of Zacchaeus (19:1–10).

Zacchaeus was by no means poor in the economic sense of the word. He was the senior tax collector in Jericho, and this had enabled him to accumulate a considerable amount of wealth, but he remained an outcast because of his profession and would have been classified as a sinner. No "respectable" person would enter his house or dine with him. Jesus quite deliberately invites himself to the house of this man—the most notorious sinner in Jericho.

But, once they had begun to get the measure of Jesus, the tax collectors and sinners, like the sick and the disabled, would have begun, as Luke tells us, to seek out his company (15:1) and invite him to meals in their homes.

Jesus himself attached great importance to these festive gatherings. He sometimes hired a dining-room in an inn to celebrate with his followers. The last supper was indeed the last of many such suppers. After his death his followers kept up his memory by continuing to break bread together. This was how he had wished to be remembered — in the context of a festive meal. "Do this in memory of me" (1 Cor 11:24, 25).

It would be impossible to overestimate the impact these meals must have had upon the poor and the sinners. By accepting them as friends and equals Jesus had taken away their shame, humiliation and guilt. By showing them that they mattered to him as people he gave them a sense of dignity and released them from their captivity. The physical contact which he must have had with them when reclining at table (compare Jn 13:25) and which he obviously never dreamed of disallowing (Lk 7:38–39) must have made them feel clean and acceptable.

Moreover, because Jesus was looked upon as a man of God and a prophet, they would have interpreted his gesture of friendship as God's approval of them. They were now acceptable to God. Their sinfulness, ignorance and uncleanness had been overlooked and were no longer being held against them.

It has often been pointed out that Jesus' table-sharing with sinners was an implicit forgiveness of their sins.[6] In order to appreciate this, one must understand how sins and how forgiveness were thought of in those days.

Sins were debts owing to God (Mt 6:12; 18:23–35). These debts had been incurred in the past by oneself or one's ancestors as a result of some transgression of the law. The transgressions could have been committed deliberately or by mistake, as we have already seen. Thus an illegitimate or racially mixed Jew was thought of as living in a permanent state of sin or indebtedness to God because of the transgression of his ancestors.

Forgiveness meant the cancellation or remission of one's debts to God. To forgive in Greek (*aphièmi*) means to remit, release or liberate. To forgive someone is to liberate them from the domination of their past history. God forgives by overlooking one's past and taking away the present or future consequences of past transgressions.

Jesus' gesture of friendship made it quite clear that this was precisely what he had in mind. He overlooked their past and refused to hold anything at all against them. He treated them as people who were no longer, if ever, indebted to God and therefore no longer deserving of rejection and punishment. They were forgiven.

It was no more necessary for Jesus to spell this out in words than it was for the father of the prodigal son to tell his son in so many words that he had forgiven him. The welcome the son received and the great feast that was put on for him spoke louder than words.

Because sickness was one of the consequences of sin, healing came to be seen as one of the consequences of forgiveness. Sickness was thought of as a punishment for sin, the price that one may be called upon to pay because of one's debt to God. If one were liberated from the sickness, it showed that one's debt must have been cancelled.[7] Thus, according to a fragment among the Dead Sea Scrolls, Nabunai, king of Babylon, could say, "I was afflicted [with an evil ulcer] for seven years and a Jewish exorcist pardoned my sins."[8]

The same idea is spelled out for the reader in the gospel story of the paralytic (Mk 2:1–12 par). If the man can get up and walk, then it shows that his sins must have been forgiven. He was probably suffering from a guilt complex, which gave rise to a psychosomatic paralysis of the body. Once Jesus had assured him that his sins were forgiven, that he was not in debt to God, his fatalistic feeling of guilt was removed and he was able to walk again.

The dialogue between Jesus and the Pharisees in this story was probably composed by Mark or an earlier Christian preacher. The purpose of the dialogue was to point out that healing can be a sign or proof of forgiveness. It does not follow from this that Jesus' *motive* for healing the paralytic was to prove his ability to forgive sin. His motive for healing, as we have seen, was compassion. His motive for assuring the paralytic of God's forgiveness was also compassion. The power to heal, as we have seen, was the power of faith. The power to forgive sins was also the power of faith. The crowds are said to have marvelled not because such powers had been given to *Jesus* but because such powers had been given to *human beings* (Mt 9:8). Anyone with sufficient faith could have done the same.

This point is made clear in the story of the sinful woman who washes Jesus' feet. " 'Your sins are forgiven,' Jesus says. . . . *'Your faith* has saved you; go in peace' " (Lk 7:48, 50).

Here the dialogue has been constructed in order to point out that it was the woman's faith that enabled God's forgiveness to become effective in her. Jesus had convinced her that all her debts had been cancelled and that God now accepted her and approved of her. The moment she believed this, it took effect and her life was transformed. Jesus' faith in God's unconditional forgiveness had awakened the same faith in her. How exactly he did it we do not know. It must have been done by means of some simple gesture of friendship and acceptance—perhaps nothing more than the fact that he allowed her to wash his feet with her tears. He had not rejected her as prophets were expected to do (Lk 7:39). He had not punished her, scolded her or treated her as unclean. Like the father in the parable of the prodigal son Jesus had imposed no conditions, no qualifications, no works and no achievements. In one simple gesture she had been totally liberated from her past—gratuitously and unconditionally .

The result was a kind of healing or salvation which she experienced as relief, joy, gratitude and love. "Her sins, her many sins, must have been forgiven her, or she would not have shown such great love" [= gratitude][9] (Lk 7:47).

Her grateful love and uncontrollable joy were a sure sign of her liberation from sin. *Joy* was in fact the most characteristic result of all Jesus' activity amongst the poor and the oppressed. The meals he had with them were festive celebrations, parties. Jesus obviously had a way of ensuring that people enjoyed themselves at these gatherings. The Pharisees were scandalized by this. Rejoicing and celebrating with sinners was incomprehensibly scandalous (Lk 15:1). They could only assume that he had become a pleasure-seeker, "a drunkard and a glutton" (Lk 7:34).

In order to explain this rejoicing and celebrating to the Pharisees, Jesus told three parables—the parables of the lost sheep, the lost coin and the lost son (Lk 15:1–32). The point of each of these parables is that the finding or recovery of what was lost (forgiveness) is a natural enough reason for rejoicing and celebrating.

There can be no doubt that Jesus was a remarkably cheerful person and that his joy, like his faith and hope, was infectious. This was in fact the most characteristic and most noticeable difference between Jesus and John. As we shall see later, Jesus feasted while John fasted (Lk 7:31–34 par).

As Schillebeeckx has so aptly put it, the fact that Jesus' disciples did not fast witnesses to the "existential impossibility of being sad in the company of Jesus."[10] Fasting was a sign of sadness and sorrow. One simply does not fast while in the company of the bridegroom at a wedding celebration (Mk 2:18–19 parr). The poor and the oppressed and anyone else who was not too hung up on "respectability" found the company of Jesus a liberating experience of sheer joy.

He made them feel safe and secure. It was not necessary to fear evil spirits, evil men or storms on the lake. They did not have to worry about how they would be clothed or what they would eat or about falling sick. It is remarkable how frequently Jesus is said to have reassured and encouraged them with words like: "Don't be afraid," "Don't worry" or "Cheer up" (Mk 5:36; 6:50; Mt 6:25, 27, 28, 31, 34; 9:2, 22; 10:19, 26, 28, 31; 14:27; Lk 12:32; Jn 16:33 and all the parallel texts; see also Mk 4:19, 40; 10:49; Lk 10:41). Jesus not only healed them and forgave them, he also dispelled their fears and relieved them of their worries. His very presence had liberated them.

## PART THREE

# GOOD NEWS

*Chapter 6*

# THE "KINGDOM" OF GOD

---

There are certain passages from Isaiah which Jesus probably used to explain his work of liberating the poor and the oppressed (Lk 4:16–21; 7:22 par; Mt 10:7–8). It seems that Luke found in his sources a story about Jesus reading Isaiah in the synagogue at Nazareth. He took this story and, inserting one of the passages from Isaiah which describe Jesus' activity so aptly, Luke placed it at the beginning of Jesus' ministry as a kind of programmatic text (Lk 4:16–21). Even if Jesus did not actually read this text and comment on it in the synagogue, Luke's assessment of the importance of these passages for understanding Jesus' praxis is surely correct.

Three passages from Isaiah should be noticed:

> The *deaf,* that day,
> will hear the words of a book
> and, after shadow and darkness
> the eyes of the *blind* will see.
> But the *lowly* will rejoice in God even more
> and the *poorest* exult in the Holy One of Israel.
> (29:18–19)

> Then the eyes of the *blind* shall be opened,
> the ears of the *deaf* unsealed,

55

> then the *lame* shall leap like a deer
> and the tongues of the *dumb* sing for joy.
>
> (35:5–6)

> The spirit of the Lord has been given to me,
> for he has anointed me.
> He has sent me to bring good news to the *poor,*
> to heal the *broken-hearted;*
> to proclaim liberty to *captives,*
> freedom to *those in prison;*
> [or: to proclaim new sight to the *blind,*
> to set the *downtrodden* free]
> to proclaim the Lord's year of favor.
>
> (61:1–2*)

The deaf, dumb, blind, lame, poor, broken-hearted, captives and downtrodden are simply different ways of referring to the poor and the oppressed. It follows that the verbs in each of these sentences are simply different ways of describing the action which God promises in relation to the poor and the oppressed. Thus healing, restoring sight and hearing, bringing joy, setting free, proclaiming liberty or favor and bringing good news are different ways of describing *liberation.* It is particularly significant that proclaiming or bringing good news has been understood as a form of liberation. Jesus' preaching must be understood in this light. It was part of his liberating activity or praxis. To evangelize or bring good news to the poor means to liberate them with the spoken word.

Isaiah and Jesus himself made use of the verb "evangelize" (*euaggelizontai:* Is 40:9; 52:7; 61:1; Lk 7:22 par). It was the early Christians who first used the noun "gospel" or "good news" (*euaggelion:* e.g. Mk 1:1, 14)[1] as a way of referring to the content or message which Jesus proclaimed to the poor and the oppressed. We call something "news" when it tells of a new event, an event which has taken place recently *or* an event which we can now feel sure will take place in the near future. We say it is "good news" when the news is hopeful and encouraging, when it tends to make people happy. Good news for the poor would then mean news that is hopeful and encouraging to the poor.

The gospel or good news which Jesus brought to the poor and the oppressed was a *prophecy*. He prophesied a future event which would be a blessing to the poor. This event was not merely the coming of God's "kingdom" but the coming of God's "kingdom" for the poor and the oppressed. "Yours is the kingdom of God" (Lk 6:20).

Jesus' basic prophecy is contained in those passages of the gospel which we call the beatitudes:

> Blessed are the poor
> because yours is the kingdom of God.
> Blessed are you who are hungry now
> because you shall be satisfied.
> Blessed are you who weep now
> because you shall laugh. (Lk 6:20–21*)

It is Luke who has preserved for us the more original form of the prophecy. Here it is still addressed to Jesus' contemporaries: you who are poor, hungry and miserable. Matthew has adapted the prophecy to the needs of his readers who were not in fact poor, hungry and miserable. He has extended the blessings and promises to anyone who is poor at heart or one in spirit with the poor, anyone who hungers and thirsts for justice, anyone who imitates the meekness or lowliness of the poor, anyone who is also sad and depressed, anyone who is persecuted for his faith in Jesus, in fact anyone who is truly virtuous (5:1–12). Matthew has turned a prophecy into an exhortation.

If great hopes for the future were awakened in the poor by Jesus' activity, even greater hopes must have been awakened by his prophetic words. But these hopes had originally nothing whatsoever to do with heaven—at least not as a place of happiness and rewards in the after-life. Heaven in the time of Jesus was a synonym for God.[2] The "kingdom" of heaven means the "kingdom" of God. Having rewards or treasures in heaven means being in the good books of God. Literally heaven was the sky, the place where God and all other spirits dwell. There was no thought of people going up into heaven after death. All dead people go into *sheol*, i.e., the underworld or the grave. Even those who believed in rewards and punishments in the after-life (before the general resurrection) pictured this as something that happened in two different departments of *sheol*. The virtuous were in the bosom of Abraham in *sheol*, and a great chasm separated them from the wicked, who were in another part of *sheol* (compare Lk 16:23–26). The Christian belief in heaven originated after the death of Jesus with the idea that he had been taken up into heaven or exalted to the right hand of God.

But the good news of the "kingdom" of God was news about a future state of affairs *on earth* when the poor would no longer be poor, the hungry would be satisfied and the oppressed would no longer be miserable. To say "Thy kingdom come" is the same as saying "Thy will be done *on earth* as it is in heaven" (Mt 6:10 par).

Many Christians have been misled for centuries about the nature of God's "kingdom" by the well-known mistranslation of Lk 17:21: "The kingdom of God is *within* you." Today all serious scholars and translators agree that the text should read: "The kingdom of God is *among* you or *in your midst.*" The Greek word *entos* can mean "within" or "among" but in the present context to translate it "within" would mean that in answer to the Pharisees' question about when the "kingdom" of God would come (17:20) Jesus told them that the "kingdom" of God was within *them!* This would contradict everything else Jesus ever said about the "kingdom" or about the Pharisees. Moreover, since every other reference to the "kingdom" presupposes that it is yet to come[3] and since the verb in every other clause in this passage (17:20–37) is in the future tense, this verse must be understood to mean that one day they will find that the "kingdom" of God is suddenly and unexpectedly in their midst.[4]

The "kingdom" of God, like any other kingdom, cannot be within a person; it is something within which a person can live. Somewhere in the background behind Jesus' use of the term "kingdom of God" there is a pictorial image. He speaks of people entering or not entering *into* the "kingdom" (Mk 9:47; 10:15, 23, 24, 25 parr; Mt 5:20; 7:21; 18:3; 21:31; 23:13; Jn 3:5). They can sit down *in* it and eat and drink *in* it (Mk 14:25; Mt 8:11–12 par; Lk 22:30). The "kingdom" has a door or a gate (Mt 7:13, 14; Lk 13:24) on which one can knock (Mt 7:7–8 par; 25:10–12 par). It also has keys (Mt 16:19; Lk 11:52) and can be locked

(Mt 23:13; Lk 13:25). The pictorial image behind this is obviously that of a house or a walled city.[5]

This is further confirmed by the fact that the "kingdom" of Satan, which is opposed to the "kingdom" of God, is explicitly referred to as a house and as a city.

"How can Satan cast out Satan? If a *kingdom* is divided against itself, that *kingdom* cannot stand. And if a *house* is divided against itself, that *house* will not be able to stand." (Mk 3:23–25 RSV)

But no one can make his way into a strong man's *house* and burgle his property ... (Mk 3:27)

"Every *kingdom* divided against itself is laid waste, and no *city* or *house* divided against itself will stand." (Mt 12:25 RSV)

The most common figure in the parables is the householder. Who features in seven different parables.[6] And in no less than six parables what takes place in the house is a festive meal.[7]

There is also a parallel between the "kingdom" and the temple.[8] The temple which Jesus will build in three days (i.e., soon) is not a temple built with human hands (Mk 14:58), it is a new community. The discovery of the Dead Sea Scrolls has revealed that the community of Qumran saw itself as a new temple, a new house of God.[9] This must surely also be the meaning of Jesus' prophetic promise to build a new temple.

The fact that his way of speaking about the "kingdom" is based upon a pictorial image of a house, a city or a community leaves no doubt about what he had in mind: a politically structured society of people here on earth. A "kingdom" is a thoroughly political notion. It is a society in which the political structure is monarchical, that is to say, it is ruled and governed by a king. Nothing that Jesus ever said would lead one to think that he might have used this term in a non-political sense.

The much quoted text, "My kingdom is not *of* this world" (Jn 18:36) does not mean that the "kingdom" is not, or will not be, *in* this world or *on* this earth. The phrase is Johannine and must be understood in terms of John's use of words. In John 17:11, 14–16, when Jesus and his disciples are said to be *in* the world but not *of* the world, the meaning is clear enough. Although they live in the world they are not worldly, they do not subscribe to the present values and standards of the world. If in the same gospel it is also said that the "kingdom" is not of this world, we must interpret it in the same way. The values of the "kingdom" are different from, and opposed to, the values of this world. There is no reason for thinking that it means the "kingdom" will float in the air somewhere above the earth or that it will be an abstract entity without any tangible social and political structure.

That it is spoken of as *God's* "kingdom" does not make it any the less political, it merely opposes it to the human "kingdom" or better still the "kingdom" of Satan.

As Jesus understood it, Satan ruled the world. It was a perverse and sinful generation (Mk 8:38 parr; 9:19 parr; Mt 12:39–45 par; 23:33–36 and compare Acts 2:40), a world in which evil reigned supreme. This was evident not only in the sufferings of the poor and the oppressed and in the power which evil spirits had over them; it was also evident in the hypocrisy, heartlessness and blindness of the religious leaders (the scribes and the Pharisees) and in the merciless avarice and oppression of the ruling classes. This was true not only of the society in which Jesus lived, it was true of all the kingdoms of the world, all the principalities and powers. They were all in the hands of Satan, who gave them over to humans to rule, provided they worshiped and obeyed Satan (Mt 4:8–10 par). They worshipped Satan by ruling in such a way that they served the purposes of evil. Satan is a spirit who rules indirectly and invisibly. Caesar, Herod, Caiaphas, the chief priests, elders, scribes and leading Pharisees were Satan's puppets. Jesus condemned all the political and social structures of the world as it was in his day. They were all evil. They all belonged to Satan.

When God's "kingdom" comes, God will replace Satan. God will rule over the whole community of humankind and confer the "kingdom" or ruling power[10] upon those who will serve God's purposes in society. All evil will be eliminated and people will be filled with the Spirit of God.

The difference is between a community of humankind in which evil reigns supreme and a community of humankind in which goodness reigns supreme. It is a question of power and the structures of power. There may be many good people in the world now, but evil still has the upper hand, Satan is still in power.

Jesus saw his liberating activity as a kind of power struggle with Satan, a warfare against the power of evil in all its shapes and forms. His healing activity was a kind of burglary of the house or "kingdom" of Satan (Mk 3:27 parr). This was possible because something stronger than Satan was at work. In the last analysis goodness is more powerful than evil. Jesus was convinced that the "kingdom" of God would eventually triumph over the "kingdom" of Satan and replace that "kingdom" here on earth.

What then of John's and Jesus' prophecy of an unprecedented catastrophe? Did Jesus expect the "kingdom" of God to come *after* the great catastrophe or *instead of* the catastrophe, as a hopeful alternative?

We need to understand more about what this "kingdom" entails before we can venture an answer to this question. The crux of the matter is the concrete practical meaning of good and evil. The measure of Jesus' insight is the measure of his understanding of the structures of evil in society and his understanding of the values which would structure the "kingdom" of God. How do the values of the "kingdom" of God differ from the values of the "kingdom" of Satan?

## Chapter 7

# THE "KINGDOM" AND MONEY

The pursuit of wealth is diametrically opposed to the pursuit of God or the "kingdom" of God. Mammon and God are like two masters. If you love and serve the one, you must of necessity reject the other (Mt 6:24 par; compare Mk 4:19 parr). No compromise is possible.

Jesus' sayings about money and possessions are frequently regarded as amongst the "hardest" in the gospels. Most Christians tend to water them down. The most astounding statement about the "kingdom" of God is not that it was near but that it would be the *"kingdom" of the poor* and that the rich, as long as they remain rich, would have no part in it (Lk 6:20–26). It is as impossible for a rich man to enter the "kingdom" as it would be for a camel (or is it a fisherman's rope?)[1] to be threaded through the eye of a needle (Mk 10:25 parr). Mark tells us that even Jesus' disciples were astounded by this (10:24, 26). What kind of "kingdom" will this be?

> "In that case," they said to one another, "who can be saved?" Jesus gazed at them. "For men," he said, "it is impossible, but not for God: because everything is possible for God." (Mk 10:26–27)

In other words it would take a *miracle* to get the rich into the "kingdom" of God. And the miracle would not be getting them in *with* all their wealth, the miracle would be getting them to give up all their wealth so that they could enter a "kingdom" of the poor. This is what the rich young man in the gospel story was asked to do (Mk 10:17–22 parr). But, because he had too little faith in the "kingdom" of God and relied too heavily upon financial security, the miracle did not take place. God's power was not able to work in him to achieve the impossible.

There will be no place in the "kingdom" of God for the rich. There will be no rewards and no consolations there for them (Lk 6:24–26). In the parable about the rich man and beggar, Lazarus, one is given no other reason why the rich man should be so dramatically excluded from all rewards except that he was rich and that he did not share his wealth with the beggar (Lk 16:19–31). This too is all that this rich man wants to warn his brothers about. But who would believe it?

It follows that setting one's heart on the "kingdom" of God and subscribing to its values entail selling all one's possessions (Mt 6:19–21; Lk 12:33–34; 14:33). Jesus expected his followers to leave everything: home, family, land, boats and nets (Mk 1:18, 20 par; 10:28–30 parr; Lk 5:11). He warns them of the need to sit down and count the cost first (Lk 14:28–33).

Something more than mere almsgiving is being demanded here. Jesus is asking for a total and general *sharing* of all material possessions. He tried to educate the people to a detachment and carefreeness about money and possessions. They should not worry about what they are to eat and how they are to clothe themselves (Mt 6:25–33 par).

> To the man who takes your cloak from you, do not refuse your tunic. Give to everyone who asks you, and do not ask for your property back from the man who robs you. . . . Lend without any hope of return. (Lk 6:29–30, 35)

> When you have a party, invite the poor, the crippled, the lame, the blind; that they cannot pay you back means that you are fortunate. (Lk 14:13–14)

But the best example of Jesus' attempts to educate the people to share what they had was the miracle of the loaves and fishes

(Mk 6:35–44 parr). This incident was interpreted by the early Church and by all the evangelists as a miracle of multiplication — although this is never explicitly said by any of them. The customary way of drawing attention to a miracle is to say that the people were amazed, astonished or dumbfounded. In this case we are not told that anyone was amazed, astonished or dumbfounded; we are told that the disciples did not understand (Mk 6:52; 8:17–18, 21).[2] The event has a deeper meaning. But the event itself was not a miracle of multiplication; it was a remarkable example of sharing.

Jesus was preaching to a large gathering of people in a lonely place. It was time to stop for a while to eat. Some had no doubt brought food, others not. He and his disciples had five loaves and two fish, but they suggested that the people be told to go and "buy themselves something to eat." Jesus says, No, "You give them something to eat yourselves." They protest but he tells the people to sit down in groups of fifty and taking the bread and the fish he tells his disciples to "share it out."

Now either Jesus told the others who had brought food to do the same within their group of fifty or else they, seeing Jesus and his disciples sharing their food, began, of their own accord, to open their food–baskets and to share the contents.

The "miracle" was that so many people should suddenly cease to be possessive about their food and begin to share, only to discover that there was more than enough to go around. There were, we are told, twelve baskets of scraps left over. Things do tend to "multiply" when you share them.

The first Christian community in Jerusalem made the same discovery when they tried to share their possessions. Luke may have given us a somewhat idealized picture of this community. Nevertheless even that would be an extremely good testimony to what the early Christians understood Jesus' intentions to be.

"The faithful together owned everything in common; they sold their goods and possessions and shared out the proceeds among themselves according to what each one needed ... they shared their food gladly and generously" (Acts 2:44–46*). This does not mean that they sold absolutely everything they had. They must have kept at least their own clothes, bedding, cooking utensils, houses and furniture. The point was that "no one said [or claimed] that anything he had was his own but everything they owned was held in common" (Acts 4:32*).

What then did they sell? "All those who were *owners of lands or houses* would sell them and bring the money from them, to present it to the apostles; it was then distributed to any members who might be in need" (Acts 4:34–35).

It is obvious that what they sold was not the houses in which they lived. They did not all live under one roof. We are told that they met together in one another's houses (Acts 2:46). What they sold must have been the houses they had rented out to others. In other words they sold their real estate, their capital or investments. These were their possessions, their surplus, the extras which they did not really need.

We have another example of this in Luke's gospel. When Zacchaeus is converted he gives away half of what he owns and undertakes to pay back four times the amount to those whom he has cheated (19:8).

This then is what selling all one's possessions means: giving up the surplus and treating nothing as your own. The result will always be that "none of their members was ever in want" (Acts 4:34).

Jesus did not idealize poverty. On the contrary his concern was to ensure that no one should be in want, and it was to this end that he fought possessiveness and encouraged people to be unconcerned about wealth and to share their material possessions. But this is only possible in a community. Jesus dared to hope for a "kingdom" or world-wide community which would be so structured that there would be no poor and no rich.

His motive here again is his boundless compassion for the poor and the oppressed. When he asks the rich young man to sell everything, it is not because of some strict and abstract ethical principle. It is because of his compassion for the poor. This comes out very clearly in the version of the same story handed down to us in the Gospel of the Hebrews. After the first part of the story, which is familiar to us, the author continues:

> But the rich man began to scratch his head, and it pleased him not. And the Lord said unto him: "How canst thou say, I have kept the law and the prophets? For it is written

in the law: Thou shalt love thy neighbor as thyself, and lo, many of thy brethren, sons of Abraham, are clad in filth, dying of hunger, and thine house is full of many good things, and naught at all goeth out of it unto them."[3]

According to J. Jeremias, this saying of Jesus has as much claim to historicity as the average saying in the four gospels.[4]

It follows that any society that is so structured that some suffer because of their poverty, and others have more than they need, is part of the "kingdom" of Satan. What Jesus thought of the kind of "virtue" that does not take this attitude to money seriously and tries to compromise between God and Mammon can be read in the sequel to the statement about God and Mammon in Luke:

The Pharisees, who loved money, heard all this and laughed at him. He said to them, "You are the very ones who pass yourselves off as virtuous in people's sight, but God knows your hearts. For what is thought highly of by men is loathsome in the sight of God." (16:14–15)

*Chapter 8*

## "THE KINGDOM AND PRESTIGE"

---

In the society in which Jesus lived, money was the second most important value. The dominant value was *prestige*. "In the oriental world to this day prestige is more important than any other factor and people will commit suicide rather than forfeit it."[1]

The society was so structured that everyone had a place on the social ladder. Nothing at all was ever said or done without taking the status or rank of the persons concerned into account. An insult from someone superior to you would be accepted, even expected! An insult from an equal would be so humiliating as to make life impossible. An insult from an inferior would simply not be tolerated. A constant recognition of status was essential. People lived off the honor and respect which others gave them.

Status and prestige were based upon ancestry, wealth, authority, education and virtue. They were signified and maintained by the way you dressed and were addressed, by whom you entertained socially and who invited you to their table and by where you were placed at a banquet or where you sat in the synagogue.

Status was just as much part of religion as it was part of social life. Even the most strict and fanatical of pious Jews, the men of Qumran, relied upon their status and rank within their religious community. The Dead Sea Scrolls abound in references to the importance of knowing one's place in the precisely detailed hierarchy of the community.[2] Rights and privileges were apportioned according to one's rank and the people who had no status at all in the society—lunatics, neurotics, the blind, the lame, the deaf, the maimed and minors—were totally excluded.[3] Life in this community was explicitly based upon the rule that "one man shall be honored more than another . . . according to whether this [his status and virtue] is great or little."[4]

Jesus roundly contradicted all this. He saw it as one of the fundamental structures of evil in the world and he dared to hope for a "kingdom" in which such distinctions would have no meaning. "Blessed are you when people hate you, drive you out, abuse you, denounce your name as criminal . . ." (Lk 6:22*). "Woe to you when the world speaks well of you . . ." (Lk 6:26*).

Jesus' criticism of the scribes and Pharisees was not primarily a criticism of their teaching but a criticism of their practice (Mt 23:1–3)—in practice they lived for the prestige and admiration given to them by others. "Everything they do is done to attract attention, like wearing broader phylacteries and longer tassels, like wanting to take the place of honor at banquets and the front seats in the synagogues, being greeted obsequiously in the market squares and having people call them Rabbi" (Mt 23:5–7; compare Mk 12:38–40 par; Lk 11:43; 14:7–11).

The same is said of their religious practices of almsgiving, prayer and fasting. These things are done ostentatiously, "in order to win the admiration of men" (Mt 6:1–6; 16–18). For Jesus this is not virtue at all, it is hypocrisy (Mt 6:2, 5, 16). The scribes and the Pharisees are like whited sepulchres, they clean only the outside of cup and dish, they appear to be good, honest men but inside they are full of hypocrisy (Mt 23:27–28). They keep the law outwardly but inwardly their motive is prestige (see also Lk 18:9–14).[5]

The hypocrites, like the rich, have had their reward already: the admiration of people (compare Mt 6:1–6, 16–18 with Lk 6:20–26). There will be no place for them in the "kingdom" (Mt 5:20). In fact anyone who is concerned about prestige or "greatness" is out of tune with the values of the "kingdom" as envisaged by Jesus.

The disciples came to Jesus and said, "Who is the greatest in the kingdom of heaven?" So he called a little child to him and set the child in front of them. Then he said, "I tell you solemnly, unless you change and become like little children you will never enter the kingdom of heaven. And so, the one who makes himself as little as this little child is the greatest in the kingdom of heaven." (Mt 18:1–4)

The child is a live parable of "littleness," the opposite of greatness, status and prestige. Children in that society had no status at all—they did not count. But for Jesus they are also people and they do count. That is why he is indignant when his disciples chase the children away. He would call them to him, put his arms around them and bless them by laying his hands on their heads. "For," he says, "it is to such as these that the kingdom of God belongs" (Mk 10:14). It will be a *"kingdom" of "children"* or rather of those who are like children because in society they are insignificant; they lack status and prestige.

There is no evidence whatsoever for the popular opinion that the image of the little child is an image of innocence, especially when this comes to mean in practice immaturity or irresponsibility. Jesus was very well aware of the immature and irresponsible perversity of children at times and he uses this very trait in a parable in which it is the Pharisees who are being compared with children—the parable of the children in the marketplace who refuse to play either the joyful game of weddings or the mournful game of funerals (Mt 11:16–17 par).

But the little child who is an image of the "kingdom" is a symbol of those who have the lowest places in society, the poor and the oppressed, the beggars, the prostitutes and tax-collectors—the people whom Jesus often called the little ones or the least.[6]

Jesus' concern was that these little ones should not be despised and treated as inferior. "See that you never despise any of these little ones" (Mt 18:10). He was well aware of their feelings of shame and inferiority and because of his compassion they were in his eyes of extraordinarily great value.[7] As far as he was concerned they had nothing to fear. The "kingdom" was theirs. "There is no need to be afraid, little flock, for it has pleased your Father to give you the kingdom" (Lk 12:32).[8] The least in the "kingdom," that is to say, the little ones,[9] are greater than the greatest man born of woman, John the Baptist (Mt 11:11 par), which is a paradoxical way of saying that even the prestige of John the Baptist is of no value in itself.

What is even more extraordinary is the contrast Jesus makes between the "babes" and the wise or intelligent (Mt 11:25 par). The scribes enjoyed a tremendous amount of honor and prestige in that society because of their education and learning. Everyone looked up to them because of their wisdom and intelligence. The "babes" or "infants" were Jesus' image for the uneducated and ignorant.[10] He is saying therefore that the truth about the "kingdom" has been revealed to and understood by the uneducated and ignorant instead of the learned and wise. For this Jesus thanks God.

However this does not mean that only those who belonged to one particular class in society would be welcome in the "kingdom." Anyone may enter if one is willing to *change* and become like these little ones (Mt 18:3), to make oneself as little as a little child (Mt 18:4). Or as Mark expresses it in the same context "he must make himself last of all and servant of all" (9:35). This means in effect that one must give up all concern about any kind of status and prestige just as one must give up all concern about money and possessions. And just as one must be willing to sell all one's possessions, so one must be willing to take the last place in society—more than that, one must be willing to be everybody's servant.

Jesus' love for the poor and the oppressed was not an exclusive love; it was an indication of the fact that what he valued was humanity not status and prestige. The poor and the oppressed had nothing to recommend them except their humanity and sufferings. Jesus was also concerned about the middle and upper classes—not because they were especially important people but because they too were people. He wanted them to strip themselves of their false values, of their wealth and prestige, in order to become real people. Jesus wished to replace the "worldly" value of prestige by the "godly" value of people as people.

A further indication of the way in which Jesus valued people as people would be his attitude to women. In the society of his time "to be born female was a disadvantage, the sign, perhaps, that an expectant mother's or father's prayers were not answered."[11] Women, like children, did not count. They could not become disciples of a scribe or members of the Sadducee, Pharisee, Essene or Zealot "parties." The woman's role was sex and motherhood.

Jesus stood out among his contemporaries (and most of his subsequent followers) as someone who gave women exactly the same value and dignity as men. He showed the same concern for the widow of Nain, Simon's mother-in-law, the woman with the hemorrhage and the Canaanite woman, as he showed for anyone else in need. He could count women among his friends and his followers (Mk 15:40–41 parr; Lk 7:36–50; 8:2–3; Jn 11:5; 20:11–18). They were his sisters and mothers (Mk 3:34–35 parr). As far as he was concerned, Mary of Bethany had chosen the better part when she sat at his feet as a disciple instead of leaving that to the men and helping Martha in the kitchen (Lk 10:38–42). Jesus had no scruples about mixing with prostitutes (Lk 7:36–50 and compare Mt 11:19 with 21:31, 32) or with unchaperoned women (Jn 4:7–27; 8:10–11). People were people and that was what mattered.

"Those who humble themselves will be exalted" is not a promise of future prestige to those who have no prestige now or to those who have given up all reliance upon prestige. It is the promise that they will no longer be treated as inferior but will receive full recognition as human beings. Just as the poor are not promised wealth but the full satisfaction of their needs — no one shall be in want; so the little ones are not promised status and prestige but the full recognition of their dignity as human beings. To achieve this a total and radical re-structuring of society would be required.

The "kingdom" of God, then, will be a society in which there will be no prestige and no status, no division of people into inferior and superior. Everyone will be loved and respected, not because of one's education or wealth or ancestry or authority or rank or virtue or other achievements, but because one like everybody else is a person. Some will find it very difficult to imagine what such a life would be like but the "babes" who have never had any of the privileges of status and those who have not valued it will find it very easy to appreciate the fulfillment that life in such a society would bring. Those who could not bear to have beggars, former prostitutes, servants, women and children treated as their equals, who could not live without feeling superior to at least some people, would simply not be at home in God's "kingdom" as Jesus understood it. They would want to exclude themselves from it.

# Chapter 9

# THE "KINGDOM" AND SOLIDARITY

Solidarity is not a biblical word but it expresses better than any other word I know one of the most fundamental concepts in the Bible—the concept frequently referred to by scholars as the Hebrew notion of collectivity. A family, tribe or nation is thought of as a kind of corporate person sometimes identified with the king, who speaks and acts on behalf of the group, and sometimes identified with the common ancestor from whom the group is descended.

The difference between the "kingdom" of Satan and the "kingdom" of God (between evil and good as Jesus understands it) cannot be understood without taking this notion of solidarity into account, not only because the two "kingdoms" can be seen as two corporate persons but because they represent two fundamentally different attitudes to group solidarity.

Derrett has shown that after prestige and money the fundamental concern of the society in which Jesus lived was group solidarity.[1] The Jews, down through the ages to our own day, have manifested a remarkable sense of solidarity. We know how they stand together and help one another, especially in a time of crisis. But, in the time of Jesus at least, it was not only national solidarity that mattered, or the solidarity of Judaism against the Gentile world. In practice they were even more concerned about group solidarities within the nation.

The basic unit that lived together as one corporate being was the family—the extended family including all one's relatives. Ties of blood (one's own flesh and blood) and of marriage (one flesh) were taken very seriously indeed. Not only were all members of the family regarded as brothers, sisters, mothers and fathers to one another but they identified themselves with one another. The harm done to one member of the family was felt by all. The shame of one affected all. Any one could say to an outsider, "Whatever you do to the least of my brothers, you do to me," or "Whenever you welcome one of my kinsmen you welcome me." To one's own kin one could say, "Whoever welcomes you welcomes me; whoever is ashamed of you is ashamed of me." Not that it was necessary to say it. It was taken for granted.

On the same principle, if one's kin had been insulted or murdered, one felt obliged to avenge the injury. The vendetta or blood-feud still existed in Jesus' time, albeit in a mitigated form.[2] The principle of "an eye for an eye and a tooth for a tooth" (Mt 5:39) still held good in those days. We associate this kind of thing with the Mafia and find it very difficult to understand. But often the only thing preventing us from experiencing solidarity in this particular way is our Western individualism.

In the time of Jesus it was not only the extended family that lived together as one corporate entity. Solidarity was also experienced with one's friends, one's co-workers and traders, one's social group and within the confines of an elitist "sect" like the Pharisees or the Essenes. "Individualism," as Derrett points out, "was unknown, except in the world of prayer."[3]

For all our Western individualism and for all our amazement at the lengths to which others take this group solidarity, we still retain, consciously or unconsciously, a tremendous amount of group loyalty and group prejudice. It varies from person to person but there are still plenty of people in the Western world who base their identity upon the loyalties and prejudices of race, nationality, language, culture, class, ancestry, family, generation, political party and religious denomination. Love and loyalty are just as exclusive as they ever were.

The point is that the "kingdom" of Satan differs from the "kingdom" of God not because they are two different forms of group solidarity but because Satan's "kingdom" is based upon the exclusive and selfish solidarity of groups whereas God's "kingdom" is based upon the all-inclusive solidarity of the human race. "You have learned how it was said: you must love your neighbor and hate your enemy. But I say this to you: love your enemies" (Mt 5:43–44).

Nothing could be more radical and revolutionary than that. Hatred of one's enemy is explicitly commanded in the Dead Sea Scrolls[4] and in the extra-biblical Book of Jubilees.[5] In the Old Testament, although there is no text which explicitly commands this, the command to love one's neighbor is always understood to exclude one's enemy. Your neighbor is never thought of as any other human being. Your neighbor is your kin, the person who is close to you, a member of your group.

> You must not slander *your own people* ... You must not bear hatred for *your brother* ... You must not exact vengeance ... against the children of *your people*. You must love *your neighbor as* yourself. (Lv 19:16–18)

In the Old Testament to love your neighbor as yourself is to experience group solidarity. Only your kinsperson is to be treated as another "self." To regard some as sisters and brothers always involves enmity toward others.

Jesus extended one's neighbor to include one's enemies. He could not have found a more effective way of shocking his audience into the realization that he wished to include all people in this solidarity of love. The saying is almost unbearably paradoxical: the natural contradiction between neighbor and enemy, between outsiders and insiders must be overlooked and overcome so that enemies become kin and all outsiders become insiders!

Jesus does not hesitate to spell out the almost inconceivable consequences:

> Do good to those who hate you, bless those who curse you, pray for those who treat you badly. (Lk 6:27–28)

> If you love those who love you, what thanks can you expect? Even sinners love those who love them. (Lk 6:32)

Group solidarity (loving those who love you) is no virtue. It is thickest amongst thieves. Jesus is appealing for *an experience of solidarity with humankind,* an experience that is non-exclusive, an experience that is not dependent upon reciprocity because it includes even those who hate you, persecute you or treat you badly.

This is not the same as being sisters and brothers in Christ: the ideal of loving one another that is given such prominence in the gospel and epistles of John or Paul's concept of the Church as the body of Christ. Being in Christ is the reciprocal or mutual love of those who share the experience of living in solidarity with all humankind and therefore with one another (1 Thess 3:12). Jesus appealed first of all for a loving solidarity which would exclude nobody at all.

Solidarity with humankind is the basic attitude. It must take precedence over every other kind of love and every other kind of solidarity. "If any man comes to me without *hating* his father, mother, wife, children, brothers, sisters, yes and his own life too, he cannot be my disciple"[6] (Lk 14:26).

The commentators always point out that because of the paucity of the Hebrew and Aramaic languages, the word "hate" is used to cover all the attitudes which are not love. Thus it could mean hating, being indifferent to, detached from, or not preferring, someone. In this context, we are told, Jesus is asking for detachment: that one should not give preference to one's family and relatives.[7] This is true but it does not do justice to the mode of thinking of Jesus and his contemporaries.

If love means solidarity then hate means non-solidarity. What Jesus is asking for is that the group solidarity of the family be replaced by a more basic solidarity with all humankind. This obviously does not mean that one's kith and kin are to be excluded—as enemies! They are included in the new solidarity because they too are human beings. Nor does this mean that one should love them any the less. It is the *basis* of the love that is being altered. They are not to be loved just because they happen to be your family and relatives but because they too are persons. They are to be loved with an inclusive love. In the end this will mean that they are loved all the more. They will be *loved,* not merely preferred.

All the other references to the family in the gospels confirm this interpretation.

The disciples "left house, wife, brothers, parents or children for the sake of the kingdom of God" (Lk 18:29). The solidarity of the family was not allowed to stand in the way of this new solidarity which characterized the "kingdom" (see also Lk 9:59–62).

In the process of replacing the artificial solidarity of the family by the solidarity of person to person, the unity of many a household would unfortunately be broken:

> Do you suppose that I am here to bring peace on earth? No, I tell you, but rather division. For from now on a household of five will be divided: three against two and two against three; the father divided against the son, son against father, mother against daughter, daughter against mother, mother-in-law against daughter-in-law, daughter-in-law against mother-in-law. (Lk 12:51–53; compare Mt 10:34–36)

The second part of this passage is a quotation from the prophet Micah, who deplores this breakdown in family solidarity as one of the sins of Israel in his time (Mic 7:6). That Jesus can quote this as an inevitable result of his mission is one of the clearest indications of a radical change of values. A new universal solidarity must supersede all the old group solidarities.

It may also be worth noting that the division or dissension within the family is described as a generation gap. Jesus' message does not divide father from mother or brother from sister, but parents from children. He seems to have expected the younger generation to accept universal solidarity, and the older generation to reject it.

What about Jesus himself? What about his relationship with his own family and with his mother in particular? The gospels leave us in no doubt that Jesus' relationship with most of his relatives was strained and tense.[8] Mark tells us that they thought he was out of his mind and felt compelled, as the solidarity of the family required, to take him in hand (3:21 compare Jn 7:5). Perhaps his mother was among these relatives. We are not told.

But we are told that she was among those who came to fetch him from the house in which he was "sitting around with the crowds" (Mk 3:31–32 parr). Perhaps she did not understand at the time what exactly he had in mind, just as Luke presents her as not understanding what he had in mind when at the age of 12 he told his parents that he remained in the Temple because he must be about his Father's business (3:41–50). Later she did come to understand (Jn 19:25–27). Several other members of the family, like James and Jude, came to believe in him only after his resurrection.[9]

Jesus was very seriously concerned that his love for his mother (or any other relative) should not be thought of as mere biological or family solidarity: "A woman in the crowd said: 'Blessed is the womb that bore you and the breasts you sucked!' But he said, 'Blessed rather are those who hear the word of God and keep it' " (Lk 11:27–28 RSV). Any particularly close and mutual solidarity between Jesus and his mother would have to be based upon the living out of God's will.[10]

Jesus himself abandoned the usual solidarity of the family in order to make "those around him" into his "brothers, sisters and mothers" (Mk 3:31–35 parr), so that whoever welcomed one of them, welcomed him (Mt 10:40; compare Mk 9:37 parr), and whatever was done to the least of them was done to him (Mt 25:40, 45).[11] And yet we are led to ask whether the solidarity about which Jesus felt so strongly was truly universal. He preached universal solidarity (love your enemies) but did he practice it? The modern Jewish author C. G. Montefiore has accused Jesus of not practicing what he preached because he did not love his enemies: the scribes and the Pharisees.[12] He does indeed seem to have sided with the poor and the oppressed against the middle-class scribes and the Pharisees. Is this loving one's enemies and living in solidarity with all humankind?

It could be plausibly argued that the vehemence of Jesus' attack upon the Pharisees was exaggerated by the gospel-writers because of the hostility between the early Church and the party of the Pharisees; but this would not answer our question. Did Jesus love the Pharisees or not?

If love is understood as solidarity, then love is not incompatible with indignation and anger. On the contrary, if one is genuinely concerned about people as people and painfully aware of their sufferings, one will of necessity be indignant and angry with people who make themselves and others suffer. Jesus was angry, sometimes very angry, with those who were ruining themselves and others, with those whose pride and hypocrisy would not allow them to listen when he warned them that they were heading for destruction and dragging everyone down with them. He was angry with them for the sake of all the people including themselves. In fact the surest proof that Jesus loved all people was this very pronounced indignation with the enemies of everyone's humanity, their own included.

If Jesus had refused to argue, discuss and mix socially with the Pharisees, then, and then only, could one accuse him of excluding them or treating them as outsiders. The gospels abound in examples of his conversations and meals with them and of his persistent attempts to persuade them. In the end it was they who excluded him; at no stage did he exclude them.

This is not to deny the very obvious fact that Jesus did side with the poor and the sinners. Jesus' solidarity with all people was not a vague, abstract attitude toward humankind in general. To love all people in general could mean to love no person in particular. In this book we have found it necessary to resort to such general concepts as "humankind," "humanity," "all people," "everyone" in order to ensure that the new solidarity is not interpreted as another kind of group solidarity. But Jesus did not make use of such vague boundless concepts.[13] He dealt with each individual person who came into his life or into his thoughts, in such a way that nobody was ever excluded and everybody was loved for their own sake and not for the sake of their ancestry, race, nationality, class, family connections, intelligence, achievements or any other quality. In this concrete, personal sense Jesus loved all people and lived in solidarity with all humankind. And for this very reason Jesus sided with the poor and the oppressed, with those who had nothing to recommend them except their humanity, with those who were excluded by others. Solidarity with the "nobodies" of this world, the "discarded people," is the only concrete way of living out a solidarity with humankind.

The acid test, however, is whether this solidarity with the poor and the oppressed is exclusive or not. To love them to the exclusion of others is to do nothing more than indulge in another group solidarity. Jesus did not do this. His special but non-exclusive solidarity with such people becomes therefore another sign of his solidarity with people as people.

There is one last difficulty. Jesus confined his activities to Israel and he instructed his disciples to do the same: "Go not to the territory of the Gentiles, and enter not the province of Samaria; but go rather to the lost sheep of the house of Israel" (Mt 10:5–6*).

Matthew also tells us that he hesitated to help a Canaanite woman, i.e., to work among the Gentiles. "I was sent only to the lost sheep of the house of Israel," he tells her (Mt 15:24). Even more shocking at first sight is Jesus' statement to the same Canaanite woman, "It is not fair to take the children's food and throw it to the dogs," which means to give Israel's food to the Gentiles (Mt 15:26 = Mk 7:27).

The point of the story, of course, is that Jesus did help this Gentile woman in the end, just as he did eventually help the Roman centurion. But why did she have to go to so much trouble to persuade him? And why did the Jewish elders have to beg him and plead with him to help a *Roman* centurion? (Lk 7:3–5).

On the other hand it is equally certain that Jesus envisaged a "kingdom" that would include "countless numbers" of Gentiles from north, south, east and west who would sit down with Abraham, Isaac and Jacob at a great banquet from which many a Jew would exclude himself or herself (Mt 8:11–12; Lk 13:28–29; 14:15–24). The Ninevites and the Queen of the South would be there to put the Jews to shame (Mt 12:41–42 par).

The ambivalence of Jesus' attitude to the Gentiles was one of those insoluble problems about which the scholars had endless arguments until Joachim Jeremias published his brilliant little book *Jesus' Promise to the Nations*. He has established the fact that the Jewish hope for the future did not exclude the Gentiles. In the end, after all the appropriate punishments had been meted out, the whole world including the Gentiles would come under the powerful rule of the true God. This was pictured, especially by the prophets, as a great pilgrimage of Gentile kings to Jerusalem, coming to pay homage to the final ruler of the world, Almighty God. The world had been ruled by a succession of empires. The present Empire of Rome would be replaced by the Empire of Israel, which is the Empire of the true God. With this in mind, the Jews, and especially the scribes and the Pharisees, were already busy with a massive missionary effort. Jeremias has also demonstrated that "Jesus came upon the scene in the midst of what was *par excellence* the missionary age of Jewish history."[14]

But surprising as it may seem, Jesus did not approve of this missionary effort: "Woe to you scribes and Pharisees, you hypocrites! You travel over sea and land to make a single proselyte [convert], and when you have him, you make him twice as fit for hell [Gehenna] as you are" (Mt 23:15*).

It was a case of "the blind leading the blind, and if one blind man leads another both will fall into a pit" (Mt 15:14*). As Jesus saw it, the Jews themselves would have to change first before they could think of going out to convert others. This is what Jesus set out to do and this is why he instructed his disciples to concentrate on Israel itself. Because there was very little time left (the great disaster was near) and because Israel had had centuries of preparation for this change, Jesus was convinced that God wanted the Jews to make the great change which would bring salvation and solidarity to all people. Just as he concentrated on the lost sheep of the house of Israel for the sake of all Israel, so he concentrated on Israel for the sake of all people. It was not a matter of group solidarity, it was what we might call a matter of strategy.

Jesus had at first thought that explaining the "kingdom" of God to the Gentiles would be a long, drawn-out process and that awakening enough faith in them to effect a cure would take up a considerable amount of time. On the whole this was presumably true. In any case Jesus felt it to be his particular calling to give food first to Israel and not to deprive them of the opportunity to make the great change (for which God had destined them) by spending the very little time that was left trying to convert Gentiles—giving the food to those for whom it was not at that critical stage intended. Hence Jesus' enormous surprise when he discovered a Canaanite woman who had great faith (Mt 15:28 par) and a Roman centurion whose faith was greater than anything he had yet discovered in Israel (Mt 8:10 par). *Jesus had not expected this.* If he had expected it he would not have hesitated to help them. Nevertheless he could not rely upon such an immediate response from every Gentile. It was strategically more important at that moment for the sake of everyone to concentrate on the house of Israel. In this Jesus was surely right even if in the end the people of Israel did not respond in the way in which he had hoped they would. The goal then as now was a "kingdom" in which all people would live together in solidarity.

We should mention in conclusion that the basis of this solidarity or love is compassion—that emotion which wells up from the pit of one's stomach at the sight of another's need. The parable of the good Samaritan is recorded by Luke (10:29–37) as an answer to the question, Who is my neighbor? The answer is not every person and any person, true as that may be in itself. The answer is a parable which is told in such a way that it leads us on to identify ourselves emotionally with a man who had the misfortune of falling among thieves. We feel his disappointment when those who are supposed to live in solidarity with him, a priest and a levite, pass by on the other side. We share his relief and his joy when an enemy Samaritan is moved with compassion to break through the barriers of group solidarity to help him in his need.[15] If we allow the parable to move us, if we allow the parable to release those deeper emotions which we have been taught to fear, we shall never again have to ask who our neighbor might be or what love might mean. We shall go and do likewise in the teeth of whatever barriers. Only compassion can teach a person what solidarity with other human beings means.

Of such is the "kingdom" of God.

# Chapter 10

# THE "KINGDOM" AND POWER

The last difference between the "kingdom" of God and the "kingdom" of Satan concerns power. Society and power are inseparable. A society must have a structure and that structure will have something to do with power. The issue of power and the structures of power (who has power over whom and who can decide what for whom) is what we today call politics.

In the time of Jesus politics was primarily a matter of who would be king or queen, who would be the monarch. Political power was in the very first place royal power or "kingship." In English we can distinguish between "*kingship*" and "*kingdom*" because we have two different abstract nouns derived from the word "king." But in Greek, Hebrew and Aramaic this is inconceivable. The Greek word *basileia* means both "kingship" and "kingdom" at the same time.[1] In fact *basileia* is also gender inclusive and therefore means royal power and the royal domain. Thus, whereas we usually translate the word *basileia* as "kingdom," in some contexts it might be better to translate it as "kingship" or royal power;[2] although even this would not be satisfactory. Royal power and the royal domain have to be thought of as one concept.

Up till now we have analyzed the *basileia* of God as if it referred only to a future domain or society. It is necessary for us to realize that the coming of God's *basileia* also means the coming of God's political power. Jesus prophesied that the divine political power of the future would be in the hands of the poor and the little ones.

> Blessed are the poor because yours is the *basileia* of God. (Lk 6:20*)

> I confer a *basileia* on you ... You will sit on thrones, to judge. ... (Lk 22:29, 30)

> There is no need to be afraid, little flock, for it has pleased your Father to give you the *basileia.* (Lk 12:32)

This is part of the whole idea that there is going to be a reversal of fortunes. The rich and mighty are going to be brought down low and the poor are going to be raised up high.

> He [God] has pulled down the mighty from their thrones and exalted the lowly. The hungry he has filled with good things, the rich sent empty away. (Lk 1:52–53*)[3]

> Blessed are the poor ... Woe to you who are rich ... (Lk 6:20, 24*)

> Everyone who exalts himself will be humbled, and the man who humbles himself will be exalted. (Lk 14:11)

However, this does not mean that in the power structure of the "kingdom" of God the oppressor and the oppressed are simply going to change places and therefore continue the oppression. Power in the "kingdom" of God will be totally different from power as it is exercised in the "kingdom" of Satan.

The power of Satan is the power of domination and oppression, the power of God is the power of service and freedom.

All the monarchies and nations of this present world are governed by the power of domination and force. The structure of the "kingdom" of God will be determined by the power of the spontaneous loving service which people render to one another.

This is how Jesus expressed it:

You know that among the pagans [Gentiles] their so-called rulers lord it over them, and their great men make their authority felt. This is not to happen among you. No; anyone who wants to become great among you must be your servant, and anyone who wants to be first among you must be slave to all. For the son of man himself did not come to be served but to serve,[4] and to give his life as a ransom for many. (Mk 10:42–45; compare the parallel texts and Mk 9:35)

There is no mistaking the two quite different ways in which power and authority are understood and exercised. It is the difference between *domination* and *service*. The power of this new society is not a power which has to *be* served, a power before which a person must bow down and cringe. It is the power which has an enormous influence in the lives of people by being of service to them. It is the power which is so unselfish that it will serve others even by dying for them.

It is interesting that Jesus characterizes the power of domination as typical of *Gentile* rulers. He must have had Caesar and Pontius Pilate in mind as well as the Gentile kings who feature in the Scriptures as oppressors of the Jews, especially the rulers of the great empires, whom Daniel describes as beast-like and inhuman (7:2–7, 17).

But Jesus was well aware of the fact that Jews could also be oppressors, no matter how foreign to Judaism this may have been in theory. He called Herod a fox, which is probably a reference to his Edomite or half-pagan background and might therefore be a condemnation of his typically pagan style of life and manner of exercising power.

He also realized that most of the Jewish leaders—the chief priests, elders, scribes and Pharisees—were oppressors. They did not have the arbitrary powers of kings and princes; the power which enabled *them* to dominate and oppress was the *law*.

The law was the rules and regulations handed down to the Jewish people both in the written word of Scripture and in the oral traditions of the scribes. For the Pharisees and many others the oral law had just as much validity and force as the written law. Both were *torah*, that is to say, God's revealed instructions to the people of Israel. There were instructions and rules about every imaginable detail of life, both secular and religious.[5]

Jesus was not opposed to the law as such, he was opposed to the way people used the law, their attitude to the law. The scribes and Pharisees had made the law into a *burden*, whereas it was supposed to be a *service*.

> They tie up heavy burdens and lay them on men's shoulders, but will they lift a finger to move them? Not they! (Mt 23:4)

> The sabbath was made for man, not man for the sabbath. (Mk 2:27)

The scribes had made the sabbath, like so many other laws, into an intolerable burden. They were using the sabbath against people instead of using it for them. The law as they saw it was supposed to be a yoke, a "penance," an oppressive measure; whereas for Jesus it was supposed to be for the benefit of people, to serve their needs and genuine interests. We have here two different attitudes to law, two different opinions about its purpose and therefore two different ways of using it. The attitude of the scribes leads to casuistry, legalism, hypocrisy and suffering. Jesus' attitude led to permissiveness whenever the needs of people would not be met by observance of the law, and to strictness whenever this would best serve their needs. The law was made for us, we were not made to serve and bow down before the law.

The sabbath, for example, was meant to free people from the burden of work so that they could rest for a while. It was not meant to prevent them from doing good, from healing or saving life (Mk 3:4; Mt 12:11-12; Lk 13:15-16) nor to prevent them from eating when they were hungry (Mk 2:23-26 parr). Jesus does not wish to quibble about the details of the law and its interpretation. He does not wish simply to subscribe to a less strict interpretation like that prevailing in Galilee or the Diaspora, nor does he wish to reject the oral law and rely only upon the written law. Jesus is objecting to the way in which the law, any law or any interpretation of it, is being used against people.

Jesus did not see himself as a legislator. He did not wish to abolish the Mosaic Law (Mt 5:17–18) in order to promulgate a new law or in order to do away with all laws. Nor did he wish to add to it or subtract from it or amend it — not one jot or tittle of it (Mt 5:18). What he wanted to do was to fulfill the law — to see to it that it fulfilled the role which God intended for it, that it achieved its purpose (Mt 5:18). A person keeps God's law only when she or he fulfills the purpose of even "the least of these commandments" (Mt 5:19). And the purpose of the law is service, compassion, love. God wants mercy not sacrifice (Ho 6:6; Mt 9:13; 12:7; see also Mk 12:33).

Casuistry exploited the law for its own selfish purposes, thereby destroying the purposes of the law itself. By quibbling about trivialities, "the weightier matters" or purposes of the law, namely "justice, mercy and good faith," were neglected (Mt 23:23). The insistence upon clean and unclean foods and the washing of hands and the imposition of these customs upon other people blinded everyone to the evil intentions of people toward one another (Mk 7:1–7, 14–23 par). The corban vow was used to evade supporting one's parents, thereby destroying the very purpose of God's commandment (Mk 7:8–13 par). The scribes had forgotten or preferred to ignore the original purpose behind most of the laws. They had made the law into an oppressive power.

The leaders and scholars of Jesus' time had first enslaved themselves to the law. This not only enhanced their prestige in society, it also gave them a sense of security. We fear the responsibility of being free. It is often easier to let others make the decisions or to rely upon the letter of the law. Some people *want* to be slaves.

After enslaving themselves to the letter of the law, such people always go on to deny freedom to others. They will not rest until they have imposed the same oppressive burdens upon everyone (Mt 23:4, 15). It is always the poor and the oppressed who suffer most when the law is used in this manner.

Jesus wanted to liberate everyone from the law — from all laws. But this could not be achieved by abolishing or changing the law. He had to *dethrone* the law. He had to ensure that the law would be our servant and not our master (Mk 2:27–28). We must therefore take responsibility for our servant, the law, and use it to serve the needs of humankind. This is quite different from licentiousness or lawlessness or irresponsible permissiveness.[6] Jesus relativized the law so that its true purpose might be achieved.

In the political structure of the "kingdom" of God, then, power, authority and law will be purely functional. They will embody the arrangements that are necessary if people are going to serve one another willingly and effectively.[7] Every kind of domination and every form of slavery will have been abolished. "For I tell you unless your righteousness [fulfillment of the law] exceeds that of the scribes and the Pharisees, you will never enter the kingdom of heaven" (Mt 5:20 RSV).

*Chapter 11*

# A NEW TIME

---

It is impossible for us today to come to a satisfactory understanding of Jesus' thinking and teaching without some appreciation of how he and his contemporaries felt about *time*. The neglect of this all-important concept of time by very many scholars or their misunderstandings of it has led to interminable disputes and insoluble problems. To take but one obvious example, the whole question of whether Jesus thought of the "kingdom" as present or future or both, and if both, then, how he related the present and the future of the "kingdom," is a totally artificial problem created by the attempt to understand Jesus' words in terms of our modern Western concept of time. The interminable discussions about eschatology or what the end of the world means in the Bible are hampered by a lack of clarity about the biblical concept of time.

Our Western way of thinking tends to emphasize time as a measurement. When we wish to refer to a particular time we make use of measurements recorded on clocks and calendars. We locate an epoch or an historical figure within two dates. Time is conceived of here as a measured and numbered empty space that can be filled with events of greater or lesser importance. This one might call *quantitative time*.

According to one of the real masters of Old Testament scholarship, Gerhard von Rad, "Today one of the few things of which we can be quite sure is that this concept of absolute time, independent of events, and, like blanks on a questionnaire, only needing to be filled up with data which will give it content, was unknown to Israel."[1]

The Hebrews spoke and thought of time as a *quality*. This is clearly and succinctly expressed in the famous passage from Ecclesiastes (3:1–8):

There is a time for everything, a time for every occupation under heaven:

A time for giving birth,
a time for dying;
a time for planting,
a time for uprooting what has been planted.
A time for killing,
a time for healing;
a time for knocking down,
a time for building.
A time for tears,
a time for laughter;
a time for mourning,
a time for dancing. . . .
A time for loving,
a time for hating;
a time for war,
a time for peace.

For the Hebrew, to know the time was not a matter of knowing the date, it was a matter of knowing what kind of time it might be. Was it a time for tears or a time for laughter, a time for war or a time for peace? To misjudge the time in which one lived might prove to be disastrous. To continue to mourn and fast during a time of blessing would be like sowing during harvest time (compare Zech 7:1–3). Time was the quality or mood of events.

This concept of time is not as foreign to us as it may at first appear to be. We still speak of good times, bad times, hard times, modern times and war-time. We say that the time is ripe for something or that an enterprise has no future. We characterize an idea as belonging to the nineteenth century. Here time is not a measurement any more, it is the quality of what is happening, the quality of a person's experience.

But the moment we think of history we return to our concept of quantitative time. We locate ourselves in the middle of a long imaginary line of time with the past *behind* us and the future *ahead* of us. The Jews of ancient times did not locate themselves anywhere, they located events, places and times and saw themselves as on a journey past these fixed points. Sacred events like Creation, Exodus and the Covenant with Moses, places like Jerusalem, Sinai, Bethel and times like the festivals and times for fasting or sowing were fixed points. The individual travelled through or past these fixed points. The people of the past had been there before them and had gone on *ahead* of them, in front of them. The people of the future would be coming up *behind* them, after them.[2] When individuals reach a fixed point, for example the Passover festival or a time of famine, they become in a sense *contemporaneous* with their ancestors and their successors who have passed or will pass through the same qualitative time. The individual's ancestors and successors share the same kind of time, no matter how many intervening years there may happen to be between them.[3]

The nature of the present time was felt to be determined either by the saving acts of God in the past (e.g., the Exodus) or by a saving act of God in the future. The latter was the special concern of the prophets. The great prophets of Israel had the task of telling the people *the meaning of the particular time in which they lived in view of a new divine act which was about to take place.*[4] They found that they were no longer able to understand the present situation in terms of anything that had happened in the past and therefore they compel the people to forget the past, to stop relying upon the past for meaning, security and salvation. Then they "shift the basis of salvation to a future action of God."[5]

This imminent future event qualifies and determines the present time, gives meaning to the whole of one's life at present and ordains what one ought to be doing or not doing. The future event is therefore decisive, definitive and final — it is the *eschaton*, or ultimate event, in relationship to their present time.

Because they do not have our Western concept of time as an abstract measurement, there is no empty space stretching out beyond the event they look forward to. For the people of that generation the future event is definitive and ultimate because it qualifies everything in their lives at that moment.

This future act of God was always seen by the prophets as a completely new and unprecedented event.[6] It represents a break with the past "which goes so deep that . . . it cannot be understood as a continuation of what went before,"[7] that is to say, it has no *qualitative* continuity with what has happened before. It will be a qualitatively new time, not a new measurement of time. To talk about the *eschaton* as beyond history, meaning beyond time as a measurement, is to confuse two very different concepts of time. Moreover if the present time is wholly determined and qualified by this new and unprecedented act of God, then the present time itself is a totally new time, a new era.

It is this that enables the prophet to foresee the future in the present. The *eschaton*, or future event of ultimate importance, must be read off "the horizon of world history"[8] or what is more generally called *the signs of the times.* The prophets were inspired to read the Word of God for their time in the signs of their time. It was this extraordinary insight into the nature of one's time that made a person into a prophet.

The message of a prophet is therefore never a timeless message based upon timeless ideas. It is a particular word spoken to a particular people in a concrete situation about the meaning of their time and about what they should or should not be doing there and then.[9] Later generations may be guided by a prophet who spoke centuries before only to the extent that they find themselves in a somewhat similar time and are, to that extent, contemporaries of the prophet. Much of the value and effectiveness of the prophet's message is derived from the relation of the message to a particular time. The idea that a message or teaching is of much greater value if it is timeless is a thoroughly Western notion based upon a Western concept of time.

The *eschaton* therefore is a real future event which will be qualitatively different from all previous events and which is the only event that can give ultimate meaning to one's present situation. The *eschaton* is a future event but, to the extent that our lives are determined and qualified by it, it is also a *contemporary event*, an event that can be seen in the signs of the times.

This does not mean that the Jews did not have any sense of history; it means that they had a different sense of history. We order past, present and future events in a long sequence on the basis of our measurement of time: numbered hours, days and years. For the Jews the one and only basis for this continuity of events was God.[10] It was God who ordained the times: a time for fasting or a time for feasting, a time of judgment or a time of salvation. The events of history were acts of God, and their sequence depended upon the free will of God.[11] The movement from one event to another or the change from one time to another could only be conceived of as a divine decision or decree. God could choose to alter God's purposes and intentions.[12] In such a scheme there is no place for blank spaces or intervening years between important events. Events get their quality and their sequence from the Lord of history.

Without this concept of God as the Lord of history, the Jews would have had no sense of history at all and no inkling of a great and glorious destiny. Conversely, without this concept of history the God of the Jews would have been no different from the gods of other nations.

This rather long introduction has been necessary in order to avoid the pitfall of introducing a Western concept of time into the thinking and teaching of Jesus.[13]

Jesus announced a totally new time and the imminence of God's final and definitive "kingdom": "The time has come, the kingdom of God is near" (Mk 1:15*).

The new time which Jesus announced was qualitatively different from the time announced only a few years before by John. Chronologically speaking, that is to say in terms of time as a measurement, there may even have been an overlapping—a few months or years during which John and Jesus were both making their respective proclamations. Nevertheless, Mark and Luke are specially concerned that we should not confuse John's time with Jesus' time. Mark makes sure of this by saying that Jesus went to Galilee and began his preaching "after John had been arrested" (1:14). Luke sees Jesus' baptism as the beginning of his ministry or his time and therefore he tells us about John's

preaching *and* John's imprisonment before he gives his account
of Jesus' baptism by John! (3:19–22).[14]

The qualitative difference between John's time and Jesus'
time is very well expressed in a short parable in Lk 7:31–35 =
Mt 11:16–19:

> The men of this generation are like children shouting to
> one another while they sit in the market place:
>> "We played the pipes for you,
>> and you wouldn't dance;
>> we sang dirges,
>> and you wouldn't cry."
>
> For John the Baptist comes not eating bread, not
> drinking wine, and you say, "He is possessed." The son
> of man comes eating and drinking and you say, "Look, a
> glutton and a drunkard, a friend of tax collectors and
> sinners." Yet Wisdom has been proved right by all her
> children.

John's mood is like the mournful tune of a funeral dirge;
Jesus' mood is like the joyful tune of a wedding dance. John's
behavior was characterized by fasting; Jesus' behavior was characterized by feasting. And yet they are not contradicting one
another. Both John and Jesus represent the actions of Wisdom
(that is to say, of God), *but* they speak to different times and
different circumstances. John's time was in fact a time for
mourning, and Jesus' time was in fact a time for rejoicing.

*Metanoia* (conversion) in John's time meant fasting and doing
penance; *metanoia* in Jesus' time was like accepting the invita-
tion to a feast (Lk 14:15–17) or like discovering a treasure or a
priceless pearl for which one happily sacrificed everything else
(Mt 13:44–46).[15] In John's time forgiveness was a future possibility dependent on baptism; in Jesus' time forgiveness was a
present reality and baptism in the Jordan was no longer necessary.

The newness of Jesus' time can hardly be exaggerated. The
new wine cannot be put into any of the old wineskins or religious
formulas, and the new cloth cannot be sewn onto the old gar-
ment with any success (Mk 2:21–22 parr). Even the greatest

human being born of woman is now out of date (Lk 7:28 par). The break with the past is complete and final. The past has expired. God has ordained a new time.

The time of John and the time of Jesus are radically different because they are determined by two radically different future events. John prophesied the judgment of God; Jesus prophesied the salvation of God. John lived off the prospect of a great catastrophe; Jesus lived off the prospect of a great "kingdom." John was the prophet of doom and Jesus was the herald of good news.

Like all the prophets Jesus had read the signs of the times. Events within his own time convinced him that the "kingdom" could come soon. What were these events?

The signs of the times for Jesus were, without doubt, his own successful activities amongst the poor and the oppressed—his own liberating praxis. "If it is by the finger of God that I cast out demons, then know that the kingdom of God has come upon you" (Lk 11:20 RSV).

The fact that God's power was at work in Jesus and his disciples, giving success to their efforts to liberate those who suffer, was for Jesus a sign of God's intentions. The power of faith was busy achieving the impossible. The armies of God were gaining ground against the "kingdom of Satan." Victory was not far off. The "kingdom" of God was coming up from behind, catching up with them and about to overtake them. In fact the future "kingdom" of God and the liberating activity of Jesus were contemporaneous. The "kingdom-power" of the future was already influencing the present situation.

The Pharisees want him to produce signs from heaven to authenticate his praxis and his words. He refuses to do this. Instead he points to the signs on earth (Mt 16:1–4; Lk 12:54–56). In answer to John the Baptist's question he says: "Go back and tell John what you hear and see: the blind see again, and the lame walk, lepers are cleansed and the deaf hear . . ." (Mt 11:4–5).

Goodness is triumphing over evil. God has relented and is no longer intent upon punishing the people. God now wants to save them. The implication of Jesus' praxis and his words is that *God has changed.* One can see it in these signs of the times.

It has often been said that Jesus had a radically new image of God. The God of Jesus is totally different from the God of the Old Testament or the God of the Pharisees—indeed the God of Jesus is quite unlike the God which most Christians worship. Jesus' praxis and his concept of the "kingdom" would not have been possible without a totally new image of God.

This is perfectly true except that it is not the way Jesus himself would have put it. He was not aware of changing the image of God. He was not aware of having any image of God at all. As Jesus would have thought of it, God had changed.[16] The God of Abraham, Isaac and Jacob was doing something totally new and unprecedented.[17] God has been moved by compassion for the lost sheep of the house of Israel. This has been portrayed by Jesus in the parables of the lost sheep and the lost coin and most of all in the parable of the lost son (Lk 15:1–32). These parables are Jesus' attempts to reveal to his opponents the signs of the times, the signs that God had been moved by compassion to a change of mind and to do something new.

The point is made most clearly in the parable of the lost son. The intention of the first part of the parable (Lk 15:11–20) is to impress upon us how much of a sinner the son had been and how much he had wronged his father. The homecoming takes a surprising turn; in the first place, because of what his father does *not* do. He does not reject and disown his son as the son himself had expected (v. 19) and as the father would have had every right to do. He does not demand that the son make amends for his sins or that he make restitution for the financial loss to the father by working as a hired servant, which is what Jesus' audience would have expected. He does not punish his son in any way at all, which offends against every current notion of justice. He does not even scold his son or demand an apology. There is not even a condescending word of forgiveness on the lips of this father. All he does is rejoice and order a feast, a celebration.

Why? Because he had been deeply moved by compassion (v. 20). Such was his concern for his son that having him back safe and sound outweighed every other consideration and was more than sufficient reason for rejoicing.

The elder son echoes the angry sentiments of Jesus' audience, the scribes and the Pharisees (v. 2). As far as they are concerned God would not act and is not acting like this.

But Jesus is sure that, whatever God may have done in former times, sinners are now treated with love and care, good is done to those who hate God and those who curse God are blessed, "for he is kind to the ungrateful and the wicked" (Lk 6:27, 28, 35). That is why the sick are being cured and sinners forgiven. It is the finger of a God who is now willing to forgive anyone freely and unconditionally.

The attention of God is now turned to human beings and their needs. God has come down from the heavenly throne, the highest position of prestige in the world, to be intimately close to men, women and children, who may now address God as *abba*.

The research of J. Jeremias[18] has placed it beyond all doubt that Jesus addressed God as *abba*, that he taught others to do the same (Lk 11:2) and that no one else had ever done this before. *Abba* does not simply mean father. It is the very intimate, familiar form of address reserved for the intimate family circle. It might best be translated "dad" or "papa." This contrasts very sharply with the attitude that makes people approach God in fear and trembling, the attitude that keeps God at a respectful distance because of God's supreme sovereignty and holiness.

However this does not mean that Jesus experienced God in exclusively male terms. The very use of the term *abba* opens up the possibility of also understanding the divine compassion as a hen gathering her chickens under her wings (Lk 13:34).

The success of the cures and of all Jesus' liberating activity showed him that God felt with those who suffer, that God wanted to live in solidarity with humanity and to use the godly power to serve them and protect them.

When the Pharisees refuse to believe this and ask for a sign from heaven, Jesus can only point to *the sign of Jonah.* That Jesus did in fact refer to the sign of Jonah is beyond dispute. Neither Matthew nor Luke knew what it meant. Both hazard a guess. Because of Jonah's three days and three nights in the belly of the whale, Matthew thought Jesus was referring to his resurrection as a future sign from heaven (12:40; but compare 16:1–4). Luke thought that "just as Jonah became a sign to the Ninevites, so will the son of man be to this generation" (Lk

11:30). But surely what is particularly relevant about the story of Jonah is that Jonah, like the Pharisees, was angry (4:1) when "God relented and did not inflict the disaster which he had threatened" (3:10). Jonah says, "I knew that you were a God of tenderness and compassion, slow to anger, rich in mercy, relenting from evil" (4:2). But Jonah, like the Pharisees, does not want God to be merciful to sinners (4:1–3). "Are you right to be angry," says God (4:4), "am I not to feel *compassion* for Nineveh ... for the simple people who cannot tell their right hand from their left?" (4:11).

This is surely what must serve as a sign to the Pharisees. God is once again relenting and feeling compassion for simple people. God has changed and that is why the times have changed. It is a new time, a break with the past; a time which can be understood only in terms of the new *eschaton*, the new definite future event—the "kingdom" of the poor and the oppressed.

Anyone who tries to read the signs of our present time must surely recognize some striking similarities. We live in a new time, a time that is qualitatively not all that different from Jesus' time. After we have passed through John's time and faced the impending catastrophe as an *eschaton* which determines what we should do or not do, perhaps we shall be able to go on, with the help of Jesus, to read the signs of our liberation in the events of recent times and recognize the new *eschaton* or decisive future event as the coming of God's "kingdom."

However, we are still in need of more clarity about how Jesus understood the coming of the "kingdom" in relation to the coming of the catastrophe.

*Chapter 12*

# THE COMING OF THE "KINGDOM"

Despite what has been said so far or, perhaps, because of what has been said so far, some may be tempted to understand Jesus and his ideal "kingdom" in purely secular terms. Why bring God into it? Jesus was deeply moved by compassion for the poor and the oppressed, and the success he had with them led him to believe that total liberation (the "kingdom") was imminent. All the God-talk would then be nothing more than the religious language in which, as a man of his time, Jesus had to formulate what was happening. Fortunately or unfortunately, the evidence cannot support such a contention. Jesus' conviction that the "kingdom" would come, that humanity could and would be totally liberated, would have been impossible without his belief in God.

In view of the extraordinarily high values that are supposed to reign supreme in this "kingdom," it should not be difficult to appreciate that its coming would be a *miracle*. It is a utopia, an impossible future world. But, what is impossible to us is possible to God. Jesus believed in and hoped for a miracle.

Although Jesus thought of the "kingdom" as a kind of house or city, he did not say that he or anyone else would *build* it.[1] This kind of "kingdom" can only come, it cannot be built. Nor can this kind of "kingdom" evolve out of the "kingdoms" or societies we already have, no matter how much they improve or progress in the future. Even the most powerful, most influential and most benign of leaders would not be able to establish a society like this. Worldly power, the power which forces its will upon others, even when applied ever so gently, could only produce something different from the total liberation and freedom that Jesus had in mind. People can be liberated from this or that form of domination but nobody can force a person to be free. All we can build are the conditions that will enable people to be free if they so choose. The "kingdom" itself cannot be achieved, it must be received—as a gift.

Nevertheless there is a power that can perform the miracle. It is not my power nor your power but it is a power that only I can release in myself and only you can release in yourself. This power is beyond you and me as individuals but it is not entirely outside of us. It is the supreme power that is behind all the powers at work in people and in nature. Most people call this power God. It does not matter what you call it. On occasion Jesus also called it God. But more often than not he referred to it in some other way. The prophets spoke only of God: God's word, God's promises and God's threats. The sayings and parables of Jesus are about life and the power at work in life and in nature. Only very infrequently does he find it necessary to mention God by name. There is something very profound and very revealing about the way Jesus has understood the almighty power usually represented by the word God.

We have already noticed that for Jesus the almighty power that achieves the impossible can be called *faith*. Faith releases within us a power that is beyond us. It was their faith that enabled the sick to be cured and sinners to be released from their sins. So too, it is people's faith that enables the "kingdom" to come.[2]

Jesus was relentless in his endeavors to awaken faith in the "kingdom" (Mk 1:15). He felt impelled to go from town to town preaching the good news (Mk 1:38; Lk 4:43). To awaken an even more widespread belief in the "kingdom," he instructed disciples and sent them out to preach (Mk 3:14; 6:7; Mt 10:7; Lk 9:2; 10:9, 11). The early Christians were convinced that the "kingdom" would come as soon as the good news had been preached to the whole world (Mk 13:10 par). Without preaching there would be no faith (Rom 10:17). Only when faith is strong enough in the world will the miracle of the "kingdom" take place.

There is the danger here of turning this into a mystique of faith. Faith is not a magical power. It is a straightforward decision in favor of the "kingdom" of God. The *metanoia* or change for which Jesus was appealing was a change of mind and heart, a change of allegiance. Seek first the "kingdom," set your hearts on it (Mt 6:33 par). Rely upon the "kingdom" for your consolations and rewards (Mt 6:4, 6, 18; Lk 6:20–25). Store up treasures for yourselves with God and the "kingdom," for where your treasure is there will your heart be also (Mt 6:19–21 par). Transfer your allegiance from one or other of the present "kingdoms" to the "kingdom" of God. Make the "kingdom" of God your priority in life and set all your hopes upon it. It is a hidden treasure or precious pearl, stake everything on it.

Faith is a radical reorientation of one's life. It admits of no compromise and no half-measures. One cannot serve two masters. One either makes the "kingdom" and its values the basic orientation of one's life or one does not. One either recognizes the "kingdom" as the *eschaton* and destiny of humankind or one does not. Faith is a decision. A wavering indecisiveness or a compromise would be a lack of faith (little faith) and that would be useless.

However, as we have already noted, the power of faith does not come from the fact that it is a firm decision or strongly held conviction. Faith derives its power from the *truth* of what is believed and hoped for. If the "kingdom" of God were an illusion, faith would be powerless to achieve anything. The world is full of strong but illusory beliefs that have only served to bring us to the brink of disaster. If the "kingdom" of God as preached by Jesus is true to life, if it is the truth about people and their needs, if it is the only thing that can bring humankind to fulfillment and satisfaction, then faith in this kind of "kingdom" can change the world and achieve the impossible. The power of faith is the power of truth.

True faith is not possible without compassion. The "kingdom" in which Jesus wanted his contemporaries to believe was a "kingdom" of love and service, a "kingdom" of human brotherhood and sisterhood in which every person is loved and respected because he or she is a person. We cannot believe in and hope for such a "kingdom" unless we have learned to be moved with compassion for our fellow-beings. God has now revealed God as the God of compassion. God's power is the power of compassion. People's compassion for one another releases God's power in the world, the only power that can bring about the miracle of the "kingdom."

What makes the "kingdom" come, then, is heartfelt compassion and hopeful faith. Today's faith, hope and love (compassion) are the seeds of tomorrow's "kingdom." Faith seems to be as small and insignificant as a tiny mustard seed (Mt 17:20 par) but without the seed of faith there would be no great mustard tree (Mk 4:30–32 parr). Yeast seems to be so powerless and yet it can make the whole batch of dough rise (Mt 13:33 par). A faith uncompromised by worldly values and concerns will most certainly produce a rich harvest (Mk 4:3–9 parr). The "kingdom" will be a miracle like the miracles of nature (compare Mk 4:30–32 parr and Mt 17:20 par).

But if the coming of the "kingdom" depends upon people's faith (the faith that includes hope and compassion), will the "kingdom" ever come? How can we be sure that there will ever be sufficient faith in the world to enable the "kingdom" to come? Or again, will the catastrophe not come long before there has been sufficient time to awaken faith throughout the world? And even if the catastrophe were delayed for a long time or if many people were to survive the catastrophe, is there any guarantee that the majority of people will *ever* come to believe in the kind of "kingdom" that Jesus preached? Widespread faith in such a "kingdom" would be as much of a miracle as the coming of the "kingdom" itself.

And yet Jesus had no doubt whatsoever that the "kingdom" would come. People's persistent unbelief may cause it to be delayed (Lk 13:6–9) but in the end it will come. The catastrophe may come first, many catastrophes may come first, but even then the "kingdom" of God will have the last word (Mk 13:7–8 parr). In the end the "kingdom" will come because sooner or later people *will* believe.

Why? Because there is a God.

To believe in God is to believe that goodness is more powerful than evil and truth is stronger than falsehood. To believe in God is to believe that in the end goodness and truth will triumph over evil and falsehood[3] and that God will conquer Satan. Anyone who thinks that evil will have the last word or that good and evil have a fifty-fifty chance is an atheist. There is a power for good in the world, a power that manifests itself in the deepest drives and forces in people and in nature, a power that in the last analysis is irresistible. If Jesus had not believed that, he would have had nothing at all to say.

Faith in the "kingdom" of God, then, is not merely a matter of subscribing to the values of the "kingdom" and vaguely hoping that it may one day come on earth. Faith in the "kingdom" is the conviction that whatever else the "kingdom" will come. And it is this conviction that will make the "kingdom" come because this conviction is true. "The truth *will* make you free" (Jn 8:32).

However, there is nothing here that guarantees that the "kingdom" will come *soon.* Faith could spread throughout the world very quickly and we could find the "kingdom" suddenly in our midst, but, on the basis of what we have said so far, it could equally well be delayed for a very long time. Nevertheless Jesus himself expected the "kingdom" to come soon. "The kingdom of God is near" (Mk 1:15; Mt 4:17; Lk 10:9, 11). In fact he seems to have expected it to come within the lifetime of his contemporaries — "before this generation has passed away" (Mk 13:30 parr; see also 9:1 parr). He is even reported as saying that his disciples would not have time to go around the towns of Israel before the "son of man" comes (Mt 10:23).

When one takes all the evidence into account including the parables and the urgency of the preaching, there is no mistaking Jesus' expectation of something in the very near future.

This is not to say that Jesus claimed to know the day and hour of its arrival. According to Mark, Jesus disclaimed any secret knowledge of the day and hour (13:32). The evidence throughout points to a divine intervention which comes suddenly and unexpectedly like a thief in the night or like a flash of lightning (Mk 13:33–37; Mt 24:42–44; 25:13; Lk 12:35–40; 17:24). Because nobody knows when it might come, people will be caught unawares. Hence the recurring exhortation to vigilance or watchfulness. The early Christians may have read more into this than Jesus had intended but Jesus was clearly opposed to any kind of calculation of the date by means of signs and portents (Lk 17:20–24).

Why then did Jesus insist on the nearness of the "kingdom"?

What is not generally noticed or averted to is that the *nearness* of some kind of divine intervention was not an original contribution on the part of Jesus. It was a common enough belief in his time. It was the belief which drove the Essenes out into the desert to prepare themselves. It was the belief which inspired the visions and calculations of the apocalyptic writers. The same belief led the Zealots to expect God to come and give them the victory over the Romans so that they could establish God's "kingdom" in Israel. John the Baptist called the people to a baptism of repentance because he too expected an imminent divine intervention—a judgment upon Israel itself. In other words hopes and expectations had reached an unprecedented pitch of intensity. The situation was fluid, war with the Romans was brewing and change was in the air. Would Israel defeat the Romans? Would the Messiah come? Was the world about to come to an end?

Jesus believed with John the Baptist that Israel was heading for destruction in the near future. *The event that was coming soon was the catastrophe.*

John's reaction to the catastrophe was negative. He tried to avert it or to save at least some from it. Jesus' reaction was positive. It was the moment of truth. The threat of imminent disaster was a unique opportunity for the "kingdom" to come. In the face of total destruction Jesus saw his opportunity of appealing for an immediate and radical change. "Unless you change you will all be destroyed" (Lk 13:3, 5*). If you do change, if you do come to believe, *the "kingdom" will come instead of the catastrophe.*

That this unprecedented crisis provided the people with an unprecedented opportunity for choosing between the "kingdom" and the catastrophe is the theme of many a parable or saying. The point of the parable of the unjust steward is that in the face of total loss he acts immediately and decisively, thereby securing his future happiness (Lk 16:1–8). On the other hand the rich fool builds bigger barns and then loses everything (Lk

12:16–20). "What does it profit a person to gain the whole world and then lose his or her life?" (Mk 8:36* parr). If the people, and especially the leaders, do not foresee the catastrophe and act accordingly they will be caught unawares like the house-holder who was asleep when the burglar came (Mt 24:43) or the man whose house fell in the storm because he had foolishly built it on sand (Mt 7:24–27). Now is the time to decide and to act not only in order to avoid total loss but also because an alternative is being offered: a great treasure, a priceless pearl, a great banquet (Mt 13:44–46; Lk 14:15–24 par). To delay now is to risk losing a unique opportunity.[4] Tomorrow may be too late.

The nearness of the "kingdom" was not a certainty, it was an opportunity. What was certain for Jesus was that *either* the catastrophe *or* the "kingdom" would come in the near future.[5] For Jesus the *eschaton*, or imminent act of God, was an either-or event. This is what qualified and determined Jesus' time as a time for decision and action, as a unique opportunity.

All the references, direct or indirect, to the nearness of the divine intervention confirm this conclusion. Jesus never consoled the poor with the thought that the "kingdom" was near, he prophesied rather that the "kingdom," whenever it comes, will be theirs. There was no guarantee that the "kingdom" would come soon. What would come "before this generation has passed away" and if this generation did not repent was the catastrophe (Mk 13:2–4, 30; Lk 13:3, 5). On the whole the imminent event is not the coming of the "kingdom" as such but the coming of the "son of man" (Mk 13:26 parr; 14:62 parr; Mt 10:23; 19:28; 24:37–39, 44 par; Lk 17:24; 21:36). Whether Jesus himself used the phrase or not,[6] the reference to the coming of the "son of man" is undoubtedly a reference to the coming of a judge (Mk 8:38 parr; Mt 10:32–33 parr; 19:28; 24:37–39 par). It is quite possible that "the son of man who is to come" is the same person as "the one who is to come," i.e., the judge of whom John the Baptist spoke. The reference in any case is to a judgment event (Mt 24:37–39 par).

On the few occasions when the "kingdom" itself is said to be near (Mk 1:15; 9:1 parr; Mt 4:17; Lk 10:11) the context makes it clear that we are dealing with a warning about an impending judgment, about an either-or event. Thus Jesus is not reported as saying, *"Rejoice,* for the kingdom of God is near"; but, *"Repent,* for the kingdom of God is near" (Mt 4:17, compare Mk 1:15 and Mt 3:2). All the references to some imminent event are *warnings.*

The same conclusion can be drawn from the "urgency" theme in the gospels. Because of the extreme urgency of the missionary preaching, there is no place for preachers who will look back after they have put their shoulders to the plow (Lk 9:62). There is no time to go home to bury one's father, i.e., to wait for him to die (Lk 9:59–60 par). There is no time for courtesy calls on one's friends or relatives (Lk 9:61; 10:4). One must travel light and quickly (Lk 9:3; 10:4 par). The urgency of the task demands that one drop everything immediately and leave nets, work, home, family and parents to follow in the footsteps of Jesus preaching the "kingdom" of God (Mk 1:20 par; 10:28 parr).

Why?

Because Israel was heading for destruction. If a great and glorious "kingdom" were guaranteed for the near future, there would have been no need for an urgent preaching campaign. There was no time to be lost because in those circumstances the only way to prevent Israel from plunging headlong into a catastrophe was to bring about a radical change of heart, a change radical enough to enable the "kingdom" to come instead of the catastrophe.

It is also true that if the "kingdom" had come instead of the catastrophe, those who did not belong to the "kingdom" would have experienced an individual and personal catastrophe. They would have found themselves in the outer darkness (Mt 8:12; 22:13; 25:30) bereft of all that they had treasured most in life. Those who had relied upon money, prestige, group solidarity and power for happiness and security would have found that these things had disappeared from the new world of the "kingdom." They would have experienced this as total loss, a loss of everything that had given meaning to their lives, as a destruction of their very self-hood. They would not have been excluded from the "kingdom," they would have excluded themselves.

This personal catastrophe is sometimes depicted as being in the outer darkness or as being thrown into the fire of Gehenna.

Gehenna was the name of a valley just outside Jerusalem. It was well known as the place where, centuries before, the most wicked of all deeds had been committed: children had been burned alive as human sacrifices to pagan gods (2 Chron 28:3; 33:6; Jer 7:31). It was a most unholy, contaminated, wicked place and therefore came to be used as the rubbish dump for Jerusalem. Like all rubbish dumps, it was a smelly, unhealthy place where everything was gradually decomposing and being eaten by worms and where the continuously smoldering fire, commonly found in rubbish dumps, was completing the work of destruction and corruption. The worst fate that anyone could imagine would be to be thrown onto the smoldering rubbish dump of Gehenna and left to rot away. This was the origin of the Jewish and Christian image of hell.

The imagery of fire and worms is derived from the rubbish dump of Gehenna. It should be noted that according to this imagery it is the worms that never die and the fire that is perpetual or eternal. Everything and everybody else in Gehenna dies, decomposes and is destroyed. Gehenna is the image of complete destruction, the extreme opposite of life. If Jesus used the image at all, this was what he would have had in mind. "Do not be afraid of those who kill the body but cannot kill the soul; fear him rather who could *destroy both body and soul in Gehenna*" (Mt 10:28). Hell is the destruction of the soul or the whole personality of a person: what the Book of Revelation calls the second death (2:11; 20:6, 14; 21:8). In this sense some people are already dead. "Leave the dead to bury their dead" (Mt 8:22 par). Very few of them find their way to a true and genuine life: "Enter by the narrow gate, since the road that leads to destruction is wide and spacious and many take it; but it is a narrow gate and a hard road that leads to life and only a few find it" (Mt 7:13*–14). Under the influence of the Greek idea that a soul is naturally immortal, Christians came to understand Gehenna or hell as a place of perpetual suffering for a disembodied but indestructible soul.

But it was not merely the danger of some such personal catastrophe for many of the people that made Jesus' mission so urgent. The social and political catastrophe toward which Israel was heading would engulf everyone—the innocent as well as the guilty. The innocent are seldom spared in a massacre (Mk 13:14–20). They are advised to run for their lives and "escape into the mountains" (Mk 13:14–16). The immediate urgency was to prevent *this* tragedy[7] by encouraging all the people to take the opportunity of orientating their lives toward God's "kingdom."

In the event, as we know, it was the catastrophe which came and not the "kingdom." In 70 C.E. the Romans destroyed Jerusalem and the Temple. In 135 C.E. they completed the tragedy by destroying the nation of Israel and expelling the Jews from Palestine. It was a merciless massacre causing untold suffering and loss of life.

Jesus had not been mistaken; he had failed or rather the people had failed him. A unique opportunity had been lost. But it was by no means the end. There would be another chance and still another because the "kingdom" of God will come in the end—God will have the last word. The early Christians simply adapted Jesus' prophecy to the new set of circumstances in which they found themselves.

Jesus' message, like the message of any prophet,[8] was not timeless. Nevertheless it did point to something about humanity and God that was so fundamentally and definitively true that it could be re-interpreted in relation to other times and other places. Once the message had been taken outside Palestine with its particular political crisis, and more especially once the Romans had destroyed the Jewish nation, it was felt that the message had to be adapted to other situations or indeed to any and every situation. This was done by apocalyptizing the message. It is not to my purpose in this book to argue about the merits or demerits of this process but only to notice that this is what the evangelists did with Jesus' original message.

We can see the beginnings of this process of apocalyptizing the message, even before the destruction of the Jewish nation, in the gospel of Mark.[9] "What I say to you I say to all" (13:37). The *eschaton* becomes a supra-historical event distinguishable from the historical and political catastrophe which was just about to take place (13:7, 10, 29). The supra-historical judgment on the last day is then used, in typical apocalyptic fashion, for moralizing purposes[10] and as a threat concerning the individual rather than society. Matthew takes the process very much further, laying great emphasis upon the judgment day and upon the apportioning of reward and punishment.[11]

What Jesus had to say about the last day was not apocalyptic, it was prophetic. We can recover what Jesus meant to the people of his own time, before Christianity, only by "de-apocalyptizing" the gospels.

*PART FOUR*

# CONFRONTATION

# Chapter 13

# POLITICS AND RELIGION

The most certain and well-attested fact about Jesus of Nazareth is that he was tried, sentenced and executed by the Roman procurator Pontius Pilate on a charge of high treason. This does not make him unique. Many thousands of Jewish rebels and revolutionaries were crucified by the Roman rulers of Palestine during this period. The Jews on the whole were opposed to Roman rule, and some of them, as we have seen, were intent upon overthrowing the Romans and restoring the kingdom of Israel. Jesus was found guilty of being involved in some such conspiracy and, moreover, of claiming to be the rightful king of the Jews, the heir to the throne, or what the Jews would have called the Messiah.

> We found this man inciting our people to revolt; opposing payment of tribute to Caesar; claiming to be Christ [Messiah], a king. . . . (Lk 23:2)

The inscription above his cross (The King of the Jews) leaves no doubt about the charge that was brought against him.

Was he or was he not guilty? Did he incite the people to revolt? Did he oppose payment of taxes to the Romans? Did he claim to be the king or Messiah who should be ruling over the Jews instead of Herod or Pilate or Caesar? Did he plan to overthrow the government?

**113**

At the one extreme we have those who maintain that he was guilty (at least as far as the Roman authorities were concerned) because he did claim to be the Messiah and he did want to start a violent revolution to overthrow the Roman imperialists. It is argued that Jesus was deeply involved in the politics of the time and that he started a religio-political movement not unlike that of the Zealots.[1] The similarities between Jesus and the Zealots are heavily underlined. One of the twelve was known as Simon the Zealot (Lk 6:15; Acts 1:13) and it is sometimes argued that Peter, Judas and even the sons of Zebedee were also Zealots. Moreover, some years after Jesus' death, a leading Pharisee who actually wanted to give the Jesus movement a chance, nevertheless presumed that it was something like the Zealot movement of Judas the Galilean (Acts 5:34–39). At one stage Paul was mistaken for a well-known Jewish revolutionary leader from Egypt (Acts 21:37–38).

At the other extreme we have those who maintain that Jesus was completely innocent of those political charges. He did not wish to incite the people to revolt, he told them to pay their taxes, he was a pacifist and he claimed to be the "spiritual" Messiah or "spiritual" king of the Jews. It is argued that Jesus had nothing to do with the politics of the time, that he preached a purely spiritual and religious message and that the political charges were fabricated by the Jewish leaders who wanted to do away with him.

The truth does not lie somewhere in between these two extremes. The truth of the matter is that both views are anachronistic, they are both reading later conceptions back into the situation and events of the past.

The Jews made no distinction at all between politics and religion. Issues which we would today classify as political, social, economic or religious would all have been thought of in terms of God and the law. A purely secular problem would have been inconceivable. A cursory glance at the Old Testament alone ought to make this quite clear.

Nevertheless it is possible for us to say that some of the issues of the time were what *we* would call political, provided we remember that for the Jews of that time these issues would have been conceived in terms of their religion. In this sense it is possible to say that the relationship of Israel to the imperial power of Rome was a political issue or, if you like, a religio-political issue. If Jesus differed from the Zealots on this matter, he could not possibly have done so merely because he wanted to keep out of politics. For the Jews it was a religious matter and a religious person would be expected to have an opinion about it just as much as they would be expected to have an opinion about the sabbath or about fasting (see Mk 12:13–17 parr).

Jesus wanted Israel to be liberated from Roman imperialism just as much as the Zealots, Pharisees, Essenes or anyone else wanted it. The gospel-writers however were not particularly interested in Jesus' opinion on this issue, because it did not concern those who lived outside Palestine and because, after the fall of Jerusalem in 70 C.E., it was no longer a relevant issue for anyone. But Luke, who wanted to go back to the original sources (Lk 1:1–4), made use of a document which must have been written in Palestine before the fall of Jerusalem. The scholars call this document Proto-Luke, and they maintain that very many passages in the gospel of Luke and in the Acts of the Apostles were taken from this source.[2] What interests us here is that Proto-Luke, unlike most other sources, refers constantly to *the political liberation of Israel.*

In Proto-Luke the people who feature in Jesus' birth and early childhood are referred to as "all who looked forward to the *liberation* of Jerusalem" (2:38*) or "the *consolation* of Israel" (2:25 RSV). The prophecy of Zechariah (the *Benedictus*) is concerned with the God of Israel bringing *"liberation* to his people" (1:68*) and *"salvation* from our enemies, from the hand of those who hate us" (1:71*), "to make us without fear, *rescued* from the hand of our enemies" (1:74*). The enemies of Israel are without doubt the Romans (compare 19:43). The hope and expectation expressed here is that Jesus "would be the one to *liberate* Israel" (24:21*).

Jesus set out to fulfill this religio-political expectation though not in the way in which the people might have expected and certainly not in the way the Zealots attempted to fulfill it. Jesus set out to liberate Israel from Rome by persuading *Israel* to change. Without a change of heart within Israel itself, liberation from imperialism of any kind would be impossible. That had been the message of all the prophets, including John the Baptist. Jesus was a prophet and he was involved in politics in exactly the same way as all the prophets had been.

But what kind of change would liberate Israel? According to Proto-Luke in particular, Jesus went to a great deal of trouble to persuade the Jews of Palestine that their present attitude of resentment and bitterness was suicidal. He told them to read the signs of the times (12:54–56) and to judge for themselves (12:57) instead of relying upon what the Zealots and others had told them. In the context these signs are the signs of an impending catastrophe — "the clouds looming up in the west" (12:54). It is in Proto-Luke that the catastrophe is described most clearly and consistently as a military defeat for Israel in which Jerusalem will be surrounded by her "enemies" (19:43), that is to say, "by armies" (21:20), and the Roman "eagles" will gather around the carcass of Israel (17:37).[3] No assessment of the situation could have been more at variance with the expectations of the Zealots.

"Unless you change you will all be destroyed" (13:3, 5*). Because they would not be able to overthrow the Romans in a military battle, because they would not be able to win their case against their opponents, the only sensible thing to do was to be reconciled with them (12:58). As Jesus saw it, the only way to be liberated from your enemies was to love your enemies, to do good to those who hate you, to pray for those who treat you badly (6:27–28).

This is not a matter of resigning oneself to Roman oppression; nor is it a matter of trying to kill them with kindness. It is a matter of reaching down to the root cause of all oppression and domination: humanity's lack of compassion. If the people of Israel were to continue to lack compassion, would the overthrowing of the Romans make Israel any more liberated than before? If the Jews continued to live off the worldly values of money, prestige, group solidarity and power, would the Roman oppression not be replaced by an equally loveless Jewish oppression?

Jesus was much more genuinely concerned about liberation than the Zealots were. They wanted a mere change of government—from Roman to Jewish. Jesus wanted a change that would affect every department of life and that would reach down to the most basic assumptions of Jew and Roman. Jesus wanted a qualitatively different world—the "kingdom" of God. He would not have been satisfied with the replacing of one worldly kingdom by another worldly kingdom. That would be no liberation at all.

Jesus saw what no one else had been able to see, that there was more oppression and economic exploitation from within Judaism than from without. The middle-class Jews who were in rebellion against Rome were themselves oppressors of the poor and the uneducated. The people had to suffer far more on account of the oppression of the scribes, Pharisees, Sadducees and Zealots than on account of the Romans. The protest against Roman oppression was hypocritical. This is the point of Jesus' famous answer to the question about the paying of taxes to Caesar.

In practice Roman rule meant Roman taxation. For most Jews, paying taxes to the Roman overlord meant giving to Caesar what belonged to God, namely, Israel's money and possessions. But for Jesus this was a rationalization, a hypocritical excuse for avarice. It had nothing to do with the real issue.

"Is it permissible to pay taxes to Caesar or not? Should we pay, yes or no?" Seeing through their *hypocrisy* Jesus said to them, "Why do you set this trap for me? Hand me a denarius and let me see it." They handed him one and he said, "Whose head is this? Whose name?" "Caesar's," they told him. Jesus said to them, "Give back to Caesar what belongs to Caesar—and to God what belongs to God." This reply took them completely by surprise. (Mk 12:14–17)

Jesus' answer reveals not only the hypocrisy and insincerity of the question but also the real motive behind the taxation issue: greed for money. Those who ask the question are themselves in possession of Roman coins. Coins were thought of as the personal property of the ruler who issued them.[4] This coin had on it Caesar's name and his image. It is not God's money but Caesar's money! If you refuse to give back to Caesar what belongs to Caesar then it can only be because you are a lover of money. If you really wished to give to God what belonged to God, you would sell all your possessions and give the money to the poor, you would give up your desire for power, prestige and possessions.

The real issue was oppression itself and not the fact that a pagan Roman dared to oppress God's chosen people. The root cause of oppression was humanity's lack of compassion. Those who resented Roman oppression but overlooked their own oppression of the poor were lacking in compassion just as much as, if not more than, the Romans. Considered in terms of compassion the hardship of having to pay taxes to a Roman government instead of a Jewish government and the hardship of having one's religious sensibilities offended occasionally by the pagan intruder were minimal in comparison with the hardships suffered by the poor and the sinners at the hands of their rich and virtuous fellow-citizens. Both hardships needed to be removed but Jesus was much more sensitive to the hardships of the poor and the sinners. Jesus shifted the emphasis from oppression by the Romans to oppression by the Pharisees and Sadducees (and by implication, oppression by the Zealots and Essenes).

In doing this Jesus was not avoiding the political issue. For, as Segundo has pointed out, "localizing 'the political element' of the period of Jesus in the structures of the Roman Empire because that is what most resembles a modern political empire . . . is an anachronism." He goes on to explain:

> The political life, the civic organization of the Jewish multitudes, their burdens, their oppression . . . depended much less on the Roman Empire and much more on the theology ruling in the groups of scribes and Pharisees. They, and not the Empire, imposed intolerable burdens on the weak . . . so establishing the true socio-political structure of Israel. To that extent, the counter-theology of Jesus was much more political than pronouncements or acts against the Roman Empire would have been.[5]

Besides, the struggles of the Zealots had nothing whatsoever to do with genuine liberation. They were fighting for Jewish nationalism, Jewish racialism, Jewish superiority and Jewish religious prejudice. True liberation means taking up the cause of people as human beings. To love your enemies is to live in solidarity with all people and to take up the cause of people as human beings.

The revolution which Jesus wanted to bring about was far more radical than anything the Zealots or anyone else might have had in mind. Every sphere of life, political, economic, social and religious, was radically questioned by Jesus and turned upside down. Current ideas about what was right and just were shown to be loveless and therefore contrary to the will of God.

We find examples of this in the parable of the laborers in the vineyard (Mt 20:1-15) and in the parable of the prodigal son (Lk 15:11-32). The laborers who have done "a heavy day's work in all the heat" complain because others have received the same wages for working only one hour. It seems to be so unfair and unjust, in fact, so unethical. But this is not so. One denarius is a just wage for a day's work and that is what they had agreed upon. But the employer, like God, had been moved with compassion for the many unemployed he found in the market place, and out of a genuine concern for them and their families[6] he had employed them for the rest of the day and paid them a wage which was not proportionate to the work done but proportionate to their needs and the needs of their families. Those who had worked all day do not share the employer's compassion for the others and therefore they complain. Their "justice," like the "justice" of the Zealots and Pharisees, is loveless.[7] They envy the good fortune of others and, like Jonah, they regret God's compassion and generosity toward others.

Similarly, in the parable of the prodigal son, the older son who had worked faithfully for his father "all these years" and never once disobeyed his father's orders (like the Zealots and the Pharisees) is indignant when he hears that his father has killed the fattened calf and is having a celebration for his sinful brother. The older son does not share his father's compassion for the lost son. Therefore he feels that his father is being unfair.

If we have to make use of categories like politics and religion, and if we have to use them in the sense which they generally have today, we would have to say that Jesus did not criticize the

Zealots for being *too political,* he criticized them together with the Pharisees and the Essenes for being *too religious.* The Zealots were fanatically religious. It was their zeal for the law of God that drove them to assassinate Jews who betrayed their religion (and therefore their nation) and to take up arms against the pagan intruder. The Zealots wished to follow the example of Phineas, who, when he killed a Jew for sleeping with a pagan woman, was praised for his religious zeal (Num 25:6–13).[8] What led the Pharisees to persecute and oppress the poor and the sinners was religious fanaticism. The Essenes' hatred for unclean Jews was a religiously inspired hatred.

It is difficult for us to imagine the shock with which the parable of the publican and the Pharisee must have been received (Lk 18:9–14). The Pharisee is depicted as an exemplary man of religion. He does even more than is required of him by the law: he fasts twice a week. There is no suggestion that he was a hypocrite. He does not take the credit for his own virtue; he thanks God for it. The publican or tax collector on the other hand, although he asks God for mercy, makes no attempt to mend his ways and to make restitution for all the money he has stolen.

Jesus' verdict on these two men must have sounded outrageous. The sinner is pleasing to God and the virtuous man is not. Why? Because the sinner did not exalt himself and the virtuous man did. The Pharisee dared to regard himself as superior to others like the tax collector: "I am not like the rest of mankind and particularly not like this tax collector here." This is not so much a matter of pride as an inability to share God's compassion for people. Without compassion all religious practices and beliefs are useless and empty (1 Cor 13:1–3). Without compassion all politics will be oppressive, even the politics of revolution.

One of the basic causes of oppression, discrimination and suffering in that society was its religion—the loveless religion of the Pharisees, Sadducees, Essenes and Zealots, the religion of the men. And nothing is more impervious to change than religious zeal. The piety and good works of the dutiful religious man made him feel that God was on his side. He did not need God's mercy and forgiveness; that was what others needed. The sinner, on the other hand, was well aware of his desperate need for mercy and forgiveness (Lk 18:13) and of his need to change his life. When forgiveness is offered to a man who knows that he is greatly in debt, he is extremely grateful and appreciative (Lk 7:41–43, 47). Jesus soon discovered that it was the dutiful religious man, rather than the sinner or pagan Roman, who was an obstacle to the coming of the "kingdom" of total liberation.

Jesus must have seen this first of all in the response of the people to John the Baptist's prophecy. The teachers of religion were unwilling to accept the fact that Israel was heading for destruction (Mt 21:25–26, 32). Why would God want to punish them instead of the Gentiles and the sinners? The sinners, on the other hand, flocked to John for baptism because they had no reason to doubt that a catastrophe was imminent. After all they knew they were sinners.

As Jesus saw it, the loveless teachers of religion were the people who had said Yes to God and promised to obey God (Mt 21:28–31) but in the moment of crisis when a "kingdom" of compassion and brotherhood and sisterhood is being offered to them they refuse to join in the celebration (like the elder son in the parable—Lk 15:28) and they make excuses (like those invited to the great banquet—Lk 14:16–24 par). The prostitutes and other sinners had originally said No to God but in the moment of crisis when Jesus reveals God's compassion and forgiveness, they are willing to accept the "kingdom."

Surely the most surprising thing in the gospels is that Jesus preached about a religio-political "kingdom" from which the "men" of religion (Zealots, Pharisees, Essenes and Sadducees) would be excluded, or rather from which they would exclude themselves. According to Matthew, Jesus told them that "the tax collectors and prostitutes are making their way into the kingdom of God *and not you*" (Mt 21:31).[9] It must have seemed like a "violation" of all justice and fairness that the "sons of the kingdom" should be left outside (Mt 8:12 par) while God's "enemies," the sinners and pagans, were rushing forward and pressing their way in. This was surely also the original meaning of Jesus' enigmatic statement:

> The law and the prophets reigned until John. From this time onwards the kingdom of God is proclaimed and eve-

ryone is getting in by violence [= and everyone is urgently pressed into it].¹⁰ (Lk 16:16*)

From the days of John the Baptist until now, the kingdom of heaven has been subjected to violence [= is under urgent pressure] and men of violence [= those pushing their way in] are taking it by storm. For the law and the prophets spoke out for the time until John. (Mt 11:12)

Violence here does not mean bloodshed and the use of weapons. It means not using the normal channels — the law and the prophets. The image is that of crowds of people (everyone and anyone) storming into a city in a way which appears to the rightful citizens (the Pharisees) to be illegal and unfair.

Jesus' social mixing with sinners in the name of God and his confidence that they had God's approval while the virtuous did not were a "violation" of all that God and religion and virtue and justice had ever meant. But then Jesus was not busy with a religious revival; he was busy with a revolution — a revolution in religion, in politics and in everything else.

It would have been impossible for the "men" of Jesus' time to have thought of him as an eminently religious man who steered clear of politics and revolution. They would have seen him as a blasphemously irreligious man who under the cloak of religion was undermining all the values upon which religion, politics, economics and society were based. He was a dangerous and subtly subversive revolutionary.

But what would the Romans have thought of all this? Would they have regarded it as an obscure difference of opinion among the "natives" of this particular colony? In fact had the matter come to their notice at all?

Jesus disapproved of Roman oppression just as much as any Jew did, albeit for different reasons. He disapproved of their way of "making their authority felt" and their way of "lording it over their subjects" (Mk 10:42). But he envisaged changing this by changing Israel so that Israel could present the Romans with a living example of the values and ideals of the "kingdom." He did not think that confronting the Romans with the "kingdom" of God immediately and directly would succeed in awakening in them the necessary compassion and faith.

However, Jesus did eventually feel that it would be necessary to confront those Jews who collaborated with Rome: the chief priests and elders, the leaders of the people, who belonged to the party of the Sadducees. Up till now Jesus had criticized the *men of religion*, especially the scribes and Pharisees; now he must confront the *men of affairs*, the Jewish authorities in Jerusalem. Not so much because they collaborated with Rome but because they exploited the poor. We must now take up the story of this confrontation — the confrontation which brought him to a violent death.

# Chapter 14

# THE INCIDENT IN THE TEMPLE

---

All the evidence points to a definite, though somewhat mysterious, *turning point* in the life of Jesus. Although the gospels and the traditions behind the gospels are not particularly concerned about historical cause and effect, they are all aware of a change in the situation somewhere along the way. Their interest in this change is theological rather than historical. Each writer wishes us to understand that the opposition to Jesus on the part of the leaders of Judaism reached a climax and that at the same time the messianic expectations of many of the people came to be concentrated definitely upon Jesus; while he himself at this point withdrew to a lonely place with his disciples, gave more attention to their instruction and prepared to go to Jerusalem to die.[1]

The problem from an historical point of view is the missing link explaining how Jesus suddenly became so famous and indeed notorious. His activity and teaching were explosive enough in themselves but how did he and his intentions become sufficiently widely known to be of national concern so that the authorities would want to arrest him and the people would want to make him Messiah-king? Why did he have to withdraw and become a fugitive and what made him so sure that he and his followers would die violent deaths?

The answer has been provided by one of those rare brilliant discoveries in the history of New Testament scholarship. Etienne

Trocmé, first in an article and later in a book on Jesus,[2] has shown that the Temple incident did not take place during the last week of Jesus' life but during an earlier visit to Jerusalem. Mark's schematic approach, whereby everything that happened in Galilee is related before anything that happened in Jerusalem, has misled not only Luke and Matthew but all subsequent students of the gospels. John, who has his own schematic approach centered on Judaea and Jerusalem, places the Temple incident somewhere near the beginning of Jesus' ministry (2:13–22). John is even less interested in chronology than Mark but his placing of the incident does show that it is not necessary to associate it with Jesus' last visit to Jerusalem; it was not part of the original passion narratives.

It has always been realized that Jesus must have travelled back and forth from Galilee to Jerusalem and that he had disciples in Jerusalem and Judaea as well as in Galilee.[3] Trocmé's contribution was to show that the Temple incident occurred during an earlier visit to Jerusalem and that it provides the link that is missing from the middle of the synoptic gospels. This was the incident that made Jesus a public figure, known and discussed throughout the nation. What happened in the Temple?

The so-called "cleansing" of the Temple was not a *coup* or takeover of the Temple as a first step toward the conquering of Jerusalem, as some authors have maintained.[4] Nor, on the other hand, had it anything to do with the sacrificial rites and ceremonies which took place in the Temple,[5] nor with the vague Jewish expectation that the Temple cult would be purified by the Messiah in the last days. Jesus took action in the vast courtyard of the Gentiles and not in the Holy Place where the sacrifices were offered and he took action because of the traders and money-changers. In other words his concern, as we might well expect from what we have seen so far, was not to gain power or to purify ritual. This concern was *the abuse of money and trade.*

There is plenty of evidence outside the gospels for the existence of a roaring trade in sacrificial animals in the great courtyard of the Temple.[6] There is also evidence that the traders took advantage of the demand for clean animals for devotional sacrifices by raising the prices—sometimes to exorbitant heights.[7]

The money-changers must have been doing very well for themselves too. Every male Jew was supposed to spend a certain proportion of his income in Jerusalem[8] and most pilgrim Jews would have arrived with foreign currency. This is what Jesus saw in the Temple. This is what inflamed his anger. He was not impressed by the grandeur of the buildings and colonnades (Mk 13:1–2 parr) and he ignored the elaborate ritual and ceremony.[9] He noticed only the widow who gave her last penny (Mk 12:41–44 par) and the economic exploitation of people's devotion and piety. Here were traders and money-changers blatantly serving Mammon instead of God—with the permission, perhaps with the connivance, and possibly for the profit, of the chief priests who administered the House of God.

Jesus was determined to do something about it. His compassion for the poor and the oppressed overflowed once more into indignation and anger.

According to Mark these things came to Jesus' attention one afternoon when it was already too late in the day to do anything about it (11:11). So the next day he came back, presumably after gathering a crowd of supporters to help him. He could never have succeeded alone in expelling the no doubt very unwilling traders and money-changers. This means that Jesus' action was not unpremeditated and unplanned. It was not a momentary impulse of the kind that one later regrets.

Jesus and his supporters forced the traders and money-changers, together with their merchandise and money, out of the courtyard. According to John, Jesus used a whip (2:15). Did his followers also have whips or did they brandish swords? We do not know.

Jesus must have placed guards at the gates into the courtyard not only to prevent the angry traders from returning but also to effect his command (about which Mark informs us) that nobody should carry anything through the courtyard (11:16). The courtyard had presumably been used as a shortcut for the delivery of merchandise from one side of Jerusalem to the other.

The operation must have created an immediate uproar. It has often been asked why the ubiquitous Temple police or the Roman garrison in the fortress which overlooked the courtyard did not intervene. Were they afraid that armed intervention might spark off a riot? Or *did* they intervene? Some authors have entertained the bizarre idea that Jesus and his disciples engaged the Temple police and perhaps even the Roman garrison in battle and that for a while Jesus held out against them and maintained his control of the Temple.[10] This is historically impossible not only because it does not accord with what Jesus had said and done up till then nor with subsequent events but also because it would certainly have been recorded in the annals of the Jewish historian Josephus as an event of considerable political and military importance.

It seems to me that the Temple police probably did intervene but only for the purpose of maintaining order until the chief priests and scribes could come and negotiate a peaceful solution to the problem. In other words Jesus did not resist the police nor did they insist that the traders and money-changers be allowed to return. The problem of Jesus' right or authority to expel them was to be negotiated with the Temple officials. Hence the passage in the synoptic gospels about Jesus' authority and in John about the demand for a sign.

What authority have you for acting like this? Or who gave you authority to do these things? (Mk 11:28 parr)

What signs can you show us to justify what you have done? (Jn 2:18)

Everything would have depended upon the answer he gave to this question. He had no official authority within the system and he made no direct appeal to the authority of God as the prophets would have done. The chief priests, scribes and elders were unwilling to commit themselves on the issue of John's baptism. Jesus was similarly unwilling to commit himself on the issue of his authority. The rights or wrongs of what he had done could not be settled by an appeal to any kind of authority at all. His action had to be judged on its own merits. Authenticating signs were not necessary. Future events (the coming of a new kind of Temple or "kingdom" or the "son of man") would prove him to have been right.

It was no doubt while Jesus was preaching in the Temple,

either on this occasion or on some other visit to Jerusalem, that he spoke of the catastrophe to come as the destruction of the city and its Temple, and that he spoke of the "kingdom" as a new kind of Temple. In other words his preaching in Jerusalem followed the usual pattern: an urgent appeal for immediate change (*metanoia*), a warning about the catastrophic consequences of not changing, and a promise of a new Temple or community if there were to be an immediate change. But like the prophets of old he was understood to be prophesying against the Temple, the city and the nation and to be making ridiculous promises about a new Temple in the immediate future.

What must have worried the authorities even more was the influence he seemed to have over the people, and the number of them who seemed to believe this presumptuous Galilean of whom they had probably never heard until he created the uproar in the Temple market. Suddenly Jesus had become a figure of national importance. He could no longer be ignored. The leaders of the people would have to decide about him.

The events which led up to Jesus' execution have been handed down to us in a very confused manner indeed. But if we are to rely only upon what can be gleaned from the evidence with certainty, we would have to say that some time after the Temple incident and before Jesus was arrested, at least some of the authorities in Jerusalem conspired and decided to destroy him.

John has the famous conspiracy scene (11:47-52) in which the high priest, Caiaphas, at a meeting of chief priests and Pharisees, maintains, "It is more expedient for one man to die . . . than for the whole nation to be destroyed" (11:50*).

The details of this scene in John may not be, and were probably never intended to be, an accurate historical account of what transpired at the meeting. But the fact that there was some such conspiracy is attested by the independent account of it which we find in the other three gospels (Mk 14:1-2; Mt 26:3-5; Lk 22:2) and by the fact that at some stage Jesus became a fugitive.

Jesus must have known that they wanted to arrest him. Shortly after the Temple incident he withdrew and went into hiding (Jn 8:59; 10:39; 12:36). He could no longer move about openly (Jn 11:54) and was forced to leave Jerusalem and Judaea (Jn 7:1).

But he was not safe in Galilee either. By now Herod was also after his blood (Lk 13:31; Mk 6:14–16 par). He could no longer walk about openly in the villages of Galilee (Mk 9:30). And so he wanders about with his disciples outside Galilee: on the other side of the lake, in the regions of Tyre and Sidon, in the Decapolis and in the vicinity of Caesarea-Phillipi (Mk 7:24, 31; 8:22, 27). At one stage he returned to the far side of the Jordan (Mk 10:1; Mt 19:1; Jn 10:40). The geography here may not be all that accurate but it can hardly be doubted that Jesus wandered about outside his own country as a fugitive and exile.

When he did eventually return to Jerusalem he had to resort to undercover arrangements. His disciples were told to meet a man who would carry a pitcher of water. They were to follow him to a house where the owner would show them a room in which they were to prepare for the Passover meal (Mk 14:12–16 parr). While in Jerusalem Jesus spent the nights outside of the city in Bethany (Mk 11:11; 14:3), Ephraim (Jn 11:54) or Gethsemane (Mk 14:32 parr). During the day he sought the safety of the crowds in the temple courtyard (Lk 21:37–38). He knew that they would not dare arrest him from the midst of the crowds that gathered for the festival "lest there be a riot" (Mk 14:2 parr; Lk 20:19).

The Temple incident had forced Jesus and his disciples to change their whole way of life. One of the best indications of this was the change of attitude toward the carrying of swords:

Jesus said to his disciples, "When I sent you out without purse or haversack or sandals, were you short of anything?" "No," they said. He said to them, "But *now* if you have a purse, take it; if you have a haversack, do the same; if you have no sword, sell your cloak and buy one." (Lk 22:35–36)

Originally they had been able to rely upon the friendliness and hospitality of people. Now they were in constant danger and it would be difficult to know who could be trusted. They were wanted people. At any moment they might be recognized and caught. They would have to be prepared to defend themselves with swords![11]

We do not know how long Jesus and his disciples were "on the run." We do know that he made use of the time to instruct his disciples more thoroughly in the mystery of the "kingdom" (Mk 4:11 parr; 9:31). These instructions might *possibly* have included plans for the structure of the coming "kingdom." God would be the Ruler. Jesus would have some kind of leadership role under God. Twelve of his followers would have to take responsibility, each for a different section of the community of Israel corresponding to the original twelve tribes. "You will sit on twelve thrones, judging the twelve tribes of Israel" (Mt 19:28 = Lk 22:30). Matthew understood this saying as a reference to the last judgment. Luke did not. To judge in the Bible means to govern, and the idea here seems to be that the twelve would be governors in the "kingdom," sharing with Jesus the *basileia*, or ruling power of God (Lk 22:29–30).

Perhaps this is the context in which the twelve began to argue about who was the greatest and who would sit on his right and on his left (Mk 9:33–37 parr; 10:35–40 par). We know his answer. Those who have any kind of position of power in the "kingdom" will have to use it to serve others (Mk 9:35; 10:41–45) and they will have to make themselves as little as a child in status and rank (Mt 18:1–4).

We cannot be sure that this kind of planning of the structure of the "kingdom" took place while Jesus was a fugitive, although Mark places these "instructions" to the "twelve" during the period of wandering outside Galilee or in hiding within Galilee (7:24, 31; 8:27; 9:30, 31, 33–34, 35; 10:35–45). However, we may be sure that it was during this period that Jesus was tempted to take power into his own hands and to allow himself to be proclaimed Messiah or king of the Jews.

*Chapter 15*

# THE TEMPTATION TO VIOLENCE

---

The Jews of Palestine were hoping and praying for a Messiah. What kind of person they were expecting can be discovered from the prayers which they used to recite in the synagogue: the Psalms of Solomon and the Eighteen Benedictions. The Messiah would be a king, a descendant of David, anointed by God. He would be a powerful ruler who would "shatter unrighteous rulers," "break them to pieces . . . with a rod of iron" and "destroy the godless nations with the word of his mouth."[1] He would use his rod of iron to instill the "fear of the Lord" into every person and direct all to "the works of righteousness."[2]

It will not be necessary for us to go into the long history of this concept of a Messiah or into the peculiar expectations of some esoteric minorities. Palestinian Jewry in general was expecting a human king who would wield political and military power in order to restore the kingdom of Israel.[3]

With this in mind and remembering the kind of "kingdom" that Jesus preached, we should not be surprised to discover that on no occasion and in no circumstances did Jesus ever claim, directly or indirectly, that he was the Messiah. This is admitted today by every serious scholar of the New Testament, even by those who are inclined to be conservative.

There are a few passages in the gospels in which Jesus appears to be referring to himself as the Messiah but these are obviously the words of the evangelists, who were all convinced

**131**

that Jesus was the Messiah.[4] One of the surest indications of the historical accuracy of the gospels is their resistance of the temptation to assert that Jesus did claim to be the Messiah, and their faithful handing on of the memory that he forbade people to proclaim him as Messiah.[5]

This was the origin of the so-called Messianic Secret. It may be possible to argue that Jesus was just secretive and non-committal about his Messiahship but more fundamentally he seems to have regarded it as a temptation of Satan which had to be rejected.

There were two incidents during this period of withdrawal and hiding which would seem to have been originally temptations to accept the kingship of Israel. The first came from four or five thousand men, the second came from Peter.

It seems that between four and five thousand men (without women and children) came out from Galilee into the lonely, deserted hills near Bethsaida to see Jesus and his disciples. Why did they come? Why did only the men come? Who organized the meeting? How did they arrange for so many to come at the same time?

There can be no doubt at all that this meeting did take place. All the gospels and all the sources and all the traditions record it. Their interest in the incident, however, was due to the later significance of the miracle of the loaves and the fishes.

The clue to the original purpose and significance of the meeting can be found in a few incidental statements. Mark tells us that Jesus sympathized with these thousands and thousands of men because they were "like sheep without a shepherd" and so "Jesus set himself to teach them at some length" (6:34). We can presume that he taught them about the kind of "kingdom" God wanted for people. We have already seen how he taught them to share the food they had. According to John the incident ended with the men saying, "This really is the prophet who is to come into the world"; but then John continues, "Jesus could see that they were about to come and take him by force and make him *king*, but he escaped back into the hills by himself" (6:14–15). According to Mark (followed by Matthew) he had to "compel" his disciples to get into the boat and go on ahead while he "dismissed" the people and then went off into the hills to pray (Mk 6:45–46; Mt 14:22–23).

We do not know who organized this meeting. It is not likely to have been the Zealots. They were lying low at this stage and they were temporarily without an effective leader—sheep without a shepherd. But in the first place the Zealot leadership, like the Maccabean leadership of former times, was dynastic, that is to say, it was passed on from father to son.[6] Besides, the Zealots, as we have seen, could never have agreed with Jesus' attitudes and beliefs.

But then the Zealots were by no means the only nationalistic Jews who wanted to overthrow the Romans in order to restore the Jewish monarchy.[7] Too many authors today give the impression that all Jews who relied upon violent revolution to liberate their country from Roman imperialism were Zealots. In the end it was the Zealots who led the revolution and then everyone else joined in under their leadership. But this had not yet happened when some four or five thousand nationalistic Jews came out into the desert to persuade Jesus to be their leader. He was a Galilean, a prophet and a wonderworker with a natural talent for leadership and he had recently made a name for himself by defying the authorities in Jerusalem and "cleansing" the Temple. There may even have been some rumors that he was a descendant of David.

Jesus was not unsympathetic toward their aspirations, their desire for liberation and their need of a shepherd. But he tried to persuade them that God's ways were not the ways of human beings and that the "kingdom" of God would not be like the usual kingdoms of humans. And here too, as always, he must have appealed for a change of heart, individual conversion and faith in a new kind of "kingdom."

But his teaching and the miracle of sharing only made them all the more convinced that he was the Messiah, God's chosen king. Before the situation could get out of hand he forced his disciples to leave in a boat and dispersed the crowds. He then felt the need for solitude, reflection and prayer.

The second temptation came from Peter—somewhere near Caesarea-Philippi.

People in general had looked upon Jesus as a prophet—like

John the Baptist, Elijah, Jeremiah or one of the other prophets
(Mk 8:28 parr). But now Peter, on behalf of the other disciples,
declares that he looks upon Jesus as the Messiah (Mk 8:29 parr).
Jesus responds by giving them strict orders not to say that about
him to anyone (Mk 8:30 parr) and then he begins to tell them
that it will be his destiny to suffer rejection (Mk 8:31 parr). Peter
takes Jesus aside and rebukes him but Jesus in his turn rebukes
Peter, saying, "Get behind me, Satan! Because the way you think
is not God's but man's" (Mk 8:32–33 parr).

This must have been a very serious quarrel. Peter was angry
with Jesus for talking about rejection and failure when the
opportunity was there to seize power and become Messiah. Jesus
was angry with Peter for playing the role of Satan, the tempter,
and thinking as men usually do in terms of the power of force.

There can be no doubt that we are dealing here with an
historical event. Neither Mark nor any other early Christian
would have dared to invent such a vehement quarrel in such
strong language between Jesus and Peter. The evangelists who
believed that Jesus was the Messiah are interested in the event
primarily because of Peter's "confession" that Jesus was the
Messiah. The quarrel is understood to have been only about
Jesus' future rejection and suffering. What was originally a
"temptation" became for the early Christians a "confession of
faith." How that can have happened, we shall see later.

We should not underestimate the reality of this temptation
for Jesus. It has also come down to us in the stylized form of a
dialogue with Satan which for thematic reasons was placed with
the other temptations during the forty days in the desert (Lk
4:5–8; Mt 4:8–10). We are given to understand that Jesus had
to *struggle* with this temptation to seize power, to accept the
kingship and to rule over a new empire — "all the kingdoms of
the world." Would this not be the best way of liberating the poor
and the oppressed? Could he not exercise authority as a service
to all people *after* he had seized power by force? Would it not
be more effective to awaken faith and change the world in this
way?

Jesus was not a pacifist *in principle*. There is no evidence that
he thought force or violence should never be used, for any reason or in any circumstances. He used force (though presumably

without bloodshed) to expel the traders from the Temple. He forced his disciples to leave the meeting in the wilderness. He told them to carry swords for their own self-defense. In these circumstances he did not tell them to turn the other cheek. The injunctions to turn the other cheek and not to resist evil are often quoted out of context. In their context they are ways of contradicting the principle of "an eye for an eye and a tooth for a tooth" (Mt 5:38–39). They do not exclude violence as such, they exclude violence for the purpose of revenge. Nevertheless the "kingdom" itself could certainly not be set up by force. The problem is, could the necessary conditions for faith, conversion and liberation not sometimes, in some circumstances, call for the use of force and violence?

All we can be sure of is that Jesus decided that in his circumstances and in his time the use of force to seize power for himself (or for anyone else) would be harmful to people and therefore contrary to the will of God. The saying "Those who draw the sword will die by the sword," which Matthew found somewhere and inserted into the story of Jesus' arrest (26:52) is not, and was surely never meant to be, a timeless truth. In some circumstances one can draw the sword without dying by the sword but in the circumstances of Jesus' arrest, when he and his disciples were so outnumbered, to draw the sword was plain suicide.

Jesus was a practical and realistic man. He could see, as most of the Pharisees and Sadducees could see, that any attempt to seize power from the Romans was suicidal. To hope for a miraculous victory was to tempt God (compare Lk 4:12 par). A war with Rome could only end in a wholesale massacre of the people. This indeed was the catastrophe which Jesus feared and which he felt could be averted only by a widespread change of heart (Lk 13:1–5).

But this was surely not the only *practical* reason why Jesus refused to attempt a *coup d'etat*. To have accepted the kingship over a people who had not transferred their allegiance to the "kingdom" of God and to lead such people in battle was to play into the hands of Satan (Mt 4:8–10 par). It would have meant accepting power from Satan over a "kingdom" which was itself without any loyalty to the "kingdom" of God and encouraging them to use violence against another, albeit more godless, kingdom. Nothing could be achieved for God's "kingdom" in this way. Israel itself would have to be converted before anything of this nature could even be contemplated. Jesus would presumably have been willing to be Messiah-king if Israel had changed its ways and the "kingdom" of God had come. Messiahship would then not have been a title of honor, prestige and power but a form of service, and the Gentiles would then have been brought into the "kingdom" not by the power of the sword but by the power of faith and compassion.

Jesus was not a pacifist *in principle*, he was a pacifist *in practice*, that is to say, in the concrete circumstances of his time. We do not know what he would have done in other possible circumstances. But we can surmise that *if* there had been no other way of defending the poor and the oppressed and *if* there had been no danger of an escalation of violence, his unlimited compassion might have overflowed temporarily into violent indignation. He *did* tell his disciples to carry swords to defend themselves and he *did* clear the Temple courtyard with some measure of violence. However, even in such cases, violence would be a temporary measure with no other purpose than the prevention of some more serious violence. The "kingdom" of total liberation for all people cannot be established by violence. Faith alone can enable the "kingdom" to come.

*Chapter 16*

# THE ROLE OF SUFFERING AND DEATH

---

The Jews had had a long tradition of persecution and suffering. Theoretically the righteous person always suffered on account of his or her righteousness, and every faithful Jew was willing to die rather than disobey the law. In Maccabean times (two centuries before Jesus) many young Jews suffered and died as martyrs for the law. When the Romans first took the Temple in 63 C.E. the priests died at their posts, carrying on the routine of sacrifice rather than running for their lives.[1] The Zealots, in Jesus' time, were willing to endure any amount of torture rather than call Caesar their lord, and thousands of them were crucified by the Romans.[2] On Masada in 73 C.E. they committed suicide rather than submit to a Gentile ruler.

The prophets on the other hand had been persecuted by Jewish leaders in Jerusalem for their criticism of Israel. By the time of Jesus the figure of the prophet was being merged with that of the martyr, and legends had arisen about the sufferings and martyrdom of almost every prophet (Mt 23:29–37 par; Acts 7:52).[3]

Death in such circumstances was widely regarded as an atonement for sin — for one's own sins and for the sins of others. The early Christians did not invent the idea of martyrdom nor the idea of an atoning and redemptive death; it was part of their Jewish heritage.[4]

But what was Jesus' attitude to suffering and death?

Like the righteous, he and his disciples would have to expect persecution. Like the Zealots, they would have to be willing to take up their cross and be crucified (Mk 8:34 parr). Like the prophets, they would have to reckon with martyrdom. But there was more to it than that. Jesus had a new teaching and, in terms of that new teaching, suffering and death were closely associated with the coming of the "kingdom."

> Blessed are the poor ...
> Blessed are those who are persecuted ...
> theirs is the kingdom of heaven.
> Blessed are you when people insult you and persecute you and speak all kinds of calumny against you ... for in the same way they persecuted the prophets before you. (Mt 5:3, 10–12*)

The blessing was originally intended for the poor and the oppressed but Jesus and his disciples, because of their compassion and solidarity with the downtrodden, inevitably came to be persecuted and rejected themselves. In order to enter the "kingdom" with the poor and the oppressed, one would have to give up all one's possessions, be willing to leave home and family and sacrifice all hope of prestige, public esteem and greatness. In other words one must deny oneself (Mk 8:34 parr) and be willing to suffer.

There is a paradox here, the paradox of compassion. The one thing that Jesus was determined to destroy was suffering: the sufferings of the poor and the oppressed, the sufferings of the sick, the sufferings that would ensue if the catastrophe were to come. But the only way to destroy suffering is to give up all worldly values and suffer the consequences. Only the willingness to suffer can conquer suffering in the world.[5] Compassion destroys suffering by suffering *with* and *on behalf of* those who suffer. A sympathy with the poor that is unwilling to share their sufferings would be a useless emotion. One cannot share the blessings of the poor unless one is willing to share their sufferings.

But Jesus went much further than that. Death is paradoxical in much the same way as suffering. There is a riddle about life and death which occurs in all the traditions, in several places in the gospels and in a variety of forms (Mk 8:35 parr; Mt 10:39; Lk 14:26; Jn 12:25). It is, without doubt, based upon the words of Jesus himself.[6] A careful comparison of each of the texts enables one to conclude that the original riddle or paradox must have been simply this: *Anyone who saves his or her life will lose it; anyone who loses her or his life will save it.* One must remember that it is meant to be a riddle. To qualify it in such a way that it refers to losing one's life in this world to save it in the next world is to cease to treat it as a riddle.[7] What then does it mean?

To save one's life means to hold onto it, to love it and be attached to it and therefore to fear death. To lose one's life is to let go of it, to be detached from it and therefore to be willing to die. The paradox is that the person who fears death is already dead,[8] whereas the person who has ceased to fear death has at that moment begun to live. A life that is genuine and worthwhile is only possible once one is willing to die.

We are left with the question of what one should be prepared to die for. The Maccabean martyrs died for the law; the Zealots died to defend the sovereignty of Israel's God; other people have been willing to die for other causes. Jesus did not die for a cause. As he understood it, one should be willing to give up one's life for exactly the same reason as one gives up possessions, prestige, family and power, namely for others. Compassion and love compel people to do everything for others. But the person who says he or she lives for others but is not willing to suffer and die for them is a liar and is dead. Jesus was fully alive because he was willing to suffer and die not for a cause but for people.

The willingness to die for others should be further qualified. It is not a willingness to die for someone or for some people; it is a willingness to die for all people. The willingness to die for some people would be an expression of group solidarity. The willingness to die for humankind is an expression of universal solidarity.

Jesus' willingness to die for all people is therefore a *service* just as everything else in his life is a service, a service rendered to all people.[9] "For the son of man did not come to be served but to serve and to offer his life as a ransom for many" (Mk 10:45*). A ransom is given to redeem or liberate others. To offer one's life as a ransom is to be willing to die so that others might live. "For many" is a Hebrew and Aramaic expression which generally means "for everyone."[10] Thus at the last supper too Jesus prefigured the offering of his blood "for many" (Mk 14:24; Mt 26:28).

So far we have discussed only Jesus' willingness to die; we have not yet considered his actual death. It is easy enough to understand what it means to be willing to die for humankind but under what circumstances would one actually die for humankind? Are there circumstances in which one could *serve* the world better by dying for it than by continuing to live for it?

Jesus must have been aware of the dangerous consequences of what he was doing and saying. Herod had silenced John the Baptist, it was now rumored that he wished to silence Jesus too (Lk 13:31). After the incident in the Temple, Jesus' life was in such danger that he had to go into hiding. It was during this time that he decided to go to Jerusalem to die (Mk 8:31 parr; Lk 9:51; 13:33). Why?

Jesus seems to have been faced with the alternatives of remaining in hiding to avoid death or coming out of hiding to face death. The four to five thousand men together with Peter and the disciples wanted him to come out of hiding as the Messiah with an army or some other display of power so as to conquer his opponents in Jerusalem. But his weapon was faith, not force. His intentions were still, as they had always been, to awaken faith in the "kingdom." He could not do this very effectively by remaining in hiding but if he came out of hiding in order to preach he would sooner or later be caught and silenced—unless his death itself could become a way of awakening faith in the "kingdom."

The service which throughout his life Jesus had rendered to the sick, the poor, sinners and his disciples and which he tried to render to scribes and Pharisees and everyone else, was the service of awakening faith in the "kingdom." There was no other way of saving people from sin, suffering and the catastrophe to come. There was no other way of enabling the "kingdom" to come instead of the catastrophe. But if he was prevented from doing this, prevented from preaching or awakening faith by word and deed, what was he to do?

He was not willing to compromise by accepting the Messiah-ship and resorting to violence nor was he willing to tailor his words to suit the authorities (if it was not already too late for that). The only alternative was to die. In these circumstances death was the only way of continuing to serve humankind, the only way of speaking to the world (Jn 7:1–4), the only way of witnessing to the "kingdom." Deeds speak louder than words but death speaks louder than deeds. Jesus died so that the "king-dom" might come.[11]

All the gospels consistently portray Jesus as a man who went to his death knowingly and willingly. The words and expressions which they use, especially in the so-called "passion predic-tions,"[12] may indeed come from later reflection after his death, but the basic fact that he did go knowingly and willingly is beyond doubt.[13]

It is also significant that these "predictions" occur during the period of withdrawal and hiding, that the first "prediction" is a response to Peter's declaration that Jesus was the Messiah (Mk 8:29–33 parr) and that each of the three main "predictions" is followed by instructions about self-denial, the willingness to die, being a servant and taking the last place (see Mk 8:34–37; 9:31–37; 10:33–45 parr).

The evidence does not allow us to decide to what extent Jesus foresaw the detailed circumstances of his death. Would his dis-ciples be arrested or he alone? Several authors have maintained that Jesus spoke as if he expected (or at least did not exclude the possibility) that he and his disciples would be executed together.[14] Would he be stoned or crucified, that is to say, would he be executed by the Sanhedrin or by Pilate? Would they arrest him during the festival or after it? Would he have much of an opportunity to preach in the Temple before they caught him?

Perhaps he did foresee some of these details. He certainly seems to have suspected that Judas would inform on him. But in none of these cases is it necessary for us to resort to expla-nations based upon divine foreknowledge or special revelations about future events. The parables alone would suffice to show us what a clear insight Jesus had into the motives of people and how well he could predict what they were likely to do and say.

It remains for us to consider whether Jesus foresaw his resurrection or not. Some of the "passion predictions" conclude with a "resurrection prediction" "and after three days the son of man will rise again" (Mk 8:31 parr; 9:31 parr; 10:34 parr; see also Mk 9:9). That Jesus should have said this is not impossible. "After three days" is a Hebrew and Aramaic way of saying "soon" or "not long afterwards."[15] Most Jews at the time believed in the resurrection of the dead on the last day, and of all Jews the martyrs were most assured of rising on that day. Jesus could not have predicted that he would rise before the last day, otherwise all the confusion, doubt and surprise when he did rise would make no sense at all. In other words all that this "prediction" could mean is that Jesus as a kind of prophet-martyr expected to rise again on the last day *and* that the last day would come soon.

This interpretation is not incompatible with Jesus' beliefs and concerns but it is certainly irrelevant to all that he had been trying to do and say in his time. He probably did agree with the Pharisees against the Sadducees about the resurrection, as the gospels tell us (Mk 12:18–27). But it is surely significant that outside of these "resurrection predictions" the only time Jesus even mentions the resurrection is in answer to the Sadducees' question about the resurrection.[16] He never raises the matter of his own accord. It is not an integral part of what he wanted to say to Israel at that time and in those circumstances. Why would one talk about resurrection when people are suffering and a catastrophe is imminent and there is every hope that the "kingdom" of God might come on earth within a few years? We may therefore wonder whether Jesus did in fact make any "resurrection predictions."

This is not to say that Jesus did not believe in the resurrection. He no doubt believed in it along with many other things that the Jews of his time believed in; just as the prophets no doubt believed in many things which were not immediately relevant to their message to the people of their time. For Jesus, in his time, resurrection, like the paying of taxes to Caesar or the sacrifices in the Temple, was simply not the issue.

The situation after Jesus' death was completely different. Then, as we shall see, resurrection became the central issue.

*Chapter 17*

# THE MAN WHO EMERGES

Jesus is a much underrated man — underrated not only by those who think of him as nothing more than a teacher of religious truth, but also by those who go to the opposite extreme of emphasizing his divinity in such a way that he ceases to be fully human. When one allows Jesus to speak for himself and when one tries to understand him without any preconceived ideas and within the context of his own times, what begins to emerge is a man of extraordinary independence, immense courage[1] and unparalleled authenticity — a man whose insight defies explanation. To deprive this man of his humanity is to deprive him of his greatness.

It is difficult for us to imagine what it must have been like to differ radically from everybody else, past and present, in an age when group conformity was the only measure of truth and virtue. The immense learning of the scribes did not impress Jesus. He differed from them without hesitation even when they were far more knowledgeable about the details of the law and its traditional interpretation than he was. No tradition was too sacred to be questioned. No authority was too great to be contradicted. No assumption was too fundamental to be changed.

There is nothing in the gospels that would lead one to think that Jesus opposed everyone in a spirit of rebellion for the sake of rebellion or because he had a grudge against the world. He gives the impression throughout of a man who has the courage of his convictions, a man who is independent of others because of a positive insight which has made every possible kind of dependency superfluous.

There are no traces of fear in Jesus. He was not afraid of creating a scandal or losing his reputation or even losing his life. All the men of religion, even John the Baptist, were scandalized by the way he mixed socially with sinners, by the way he seemed to enjoy their company, by his permissiveness with regard to the laws, by his apparent disregard for the seriousness of sin and by his free and easy way of treating God. He soon acquired what we would call a bad reputation: "Look, a glutton and a drunkard." He himself relates this with what seems to be a touch of humor (Mt 11:16–19). In terms of group solidarity his friendship with sinners would classify him as a sinner (Mt 11:19; Jn 9:24). In an age when friendliness toward any woman outside of one's family could mean only one thing, his friendship with women and especially with prostitutes would have ruined whatever reputation he still had (Lk 7:39; Jn 4:27). Jesus did nothing and compromised on nothing for the sake of even a modicum of prestige in the eyes of others. He did not seek anyone's approval, not even the approval of "the greatest man born of woman."

According to Mark (followed by Matthew and Luke) even Jesus' opponents admit that he is honest and fearless: "We know that you are an honest man, that you are not afraid of anyone, because a man's rank means nothing to you, and that you teach the way of God in all honesty" (12:14).

Although this admission is made only in order to trick him into saying something rash about the payment of taxes to Caesar, it does give us some idea of the impression Jesus made upon people. His family thought he was out of his mind (Mk 3:21); the Pharisees thought he was possessed by the devil (Mk 3:22); he was accused of being a drunkard, a glutton, a sinner and a blasphemer but nobody could ever accuse him of being insincere and hypocritical nor of being afraid of what people might say about him nor of what people might do to him.

Jesus' courage, fearlessness and independence made people of that age ask again and again, "Who is this man?"[2] It is significant that Jesus never answers the question. There is no evidence that he ever laid claim to any of the exalted titles which the Church later attributed to him.

Many scholars have argued that the one title which Jesus did claim for himself was the title "Son of Man." This is not true. Not because Jesus did not refer to himself as "son of man" but because "son of man" is not a title.

A bewildering amount of research, erudition and writing has been devoted to the subject of the so-called title "Son of Man" in the gospels. The variety of conclusions that eminent scholars have come to is even more bewildering. It is difficult to find any two who agree about anything to do with the "Son of Man," except that it is a very important title. This alone would make one suspect that something must be wrong with the way the problem is being posed. Was the term "son of man" originally a title at all? The term is never used in any confession of faith; it is never predicated of Jesus nor of anyone else; in the gospels it is never found on the lips of anyone except Jesus himself; no one ever objects to its being used by Jesus, no one questions it or shows any kind of reaction to it at all. Moreover, Vermes has now shown once and for all that this Aramaic term was not a title but that it was indeed used in Galilean Aramaic as a circumlocution for oneself, that is to say, in Galilean Aramaic the speakers could, out of awe, reserve or modesty, refer to themselves as "the son of man" instead of "I."[3] Apart from this, "son of man" was also used, according to Vermes, as a synonym for "human being."[4] In other words it could be used to underline the human as opposed to the subhuman or bestial (compare Dan 7:3–7, 17–26 with 7:13).

Certain references to the "son of man" in the gospels seem to be dependent upon Daniel 7:13, "And I saw, coming on the clouds of heaven, one like a son of man."[5] It could be argued that in these texts "son of man" is being used as a kind of title for the coming judge. But it should also be noted that Jesus is here speaking of another person distinct from himself. He does not say that he is the "son of man" who will come on the clouds. Besides, many scholars today would argue that these passages were not formulated by Jesus himself but by the very early Christians.[6]

Does this mean that Jesus' use of the term was nothing more

than an idiomatic peculiarity of his mother tongue: Galilean Aramaic? Perhaps, but it is also possible to conjecture that Jesus did have something more in mind. The evidence of the gospels would seem to show that Jesus nevertheless laid great emphasis upon the Aramaic term "son of man." If we also keep in mind the emphasis which Jesus laid upon the dignity of human beings as human beings and upon the solidarity of the human race, we can submit the conjecture that Jesus' frequent and emphatic use of the term "son of man" was his way of referring to, and identifying himself with, human beings as human beings.

Thus, to say that "the son of man is master even of the sabbath" (Mk 2:28) is to say that "the sabbath was made for man not man for the sabbath" (Mk 2:27). To say that "the son of man has power on earth to forgive sins" (Mt 9:6) is to praise "God for giving such power to men" (Mt 9:8). To say that "foxes have holes and the birds of the air have nests but the son of man has nowhere to lay his head" could mean that whereas the Herods (foxes) and the Romans (birds) have a place in the present society, human beings as human beings have no place yet. Similarly to say that "the son of man will be delivered into the hands of men" (Mk 9:31) could be a reference to the paradox that those people who identify themselves with humankind will suffer violence at the hands of other human beings.

If people acquire their identity from that with which they identify themselves, then it can be said that Jesus' identity is humankind, human beings as human beings or the "son of man."

This, as I say, is a matter for conjecture. All that can be said with any degree of certainty is that, when Jesus made use of the term "son of man," he was not claiming for himself a title, an office or a rank.

In view of his explicit teaching about titles and honors, it should come as no surprise to learn that he wished to be accepted without any titles at all. How could he claim a title if he had taught:

> You must not allow yourselves to be called *rabbi,* since you have only one Teacher and you are all brothers.
>     You must call no one on earth your *father*, since you have only one Father, and he is in heaven. Nor must you

allow yourselves to be called *masters*, for you have only one Master [who is the Christ]. (Mt 23:8–10*)

The last clause in this passage has obviously been altered by Matthew or his source. As we have seen, Jesus generally avoided any reference to the Christ or Messiah. Besides, it seems quite obvious that the original intention of the saying was that God alone was their "Teacher, Father and Master."

Unless Jesus did not practice what he preached or unless he regarded himself as an exception to the rule, we would expect to find him discouraging people from calling him Rabbi or Master. There is no direct evidence that he did do this. Perhaps he felt that it would be pedantic to correct everyone who merely wished to show that they respected him as a teacher. On the other hand, perhaps he did discourage people from addressing him as Rabbi or Master and it is only to be expected that no record of it has been handed down to us. This would sound somewhat farfetched were it not for the tradition which has indeed been handed down to us that Jesus actually discouraged people from calling him good! "Jesus said to him, 'Why do you call me good? No one is good but God alone'" (Mk 10:18 = Lk 18:19).

Mark and Luke probably took this to be a piece of irony — they believed that Jesus was good because he was divine. Matthew could make no sense of it so he altered it (19:16–17). But originally Jesus was simply practicing what he preached. They wanted to call him Master but he wanted to be their servant, the one who washes their feet (Jn 13:12–15).

Jesus must have been aware of the fact that he was fulfilling the prophecies and expectations of Scripture but it does not seem to have mattered to him *who* was fulfilling them. When, according to the gospels, John's disciples ask him whether he is the one who is to come, he does not answer the question directly, he simply points to the fulfillment of Scripture in what is now happening: "The blind see again and the lame walk, lepers are cleansed ... and the good news is proclaimed to the poor" (Mt 11:4–5).

He does not say, "I give sight to the blind, I am proclaiming the good news to the poor." What matters is that this kind of thing is being done, people are being liberated and saved. Who does it is irrelevant. He wanted his disciples to go out and do the same as he had done. It never occurred to him to stop anyone, even complete strangers, from participating in the work of liberation (Mk 9:38–40 par). Jesus' only concern was that the people be liberated.

In the face of the historical evidence for Jesus' silence about titles, some very competent modern scholars have argued that Jesus claimed authority implicitly by the way he spoke and acted.[7] They argue that his independence of all other authorities and his way of saying, "But I say to you . . ." or "Amen, amen, I say to you . . ." are implicit claims to the highest and most independent authority.[8] It is even said that this is one of the assured historical facts upon which the new quest for the historical Jesus can rely and that it is the historical basis of the Christological titles.[9]

But did Jesus claim authority, any kind of authority at all, even implicitly? Would it not be closer to the truth to say that what makes Jesus immeasurably greater than any other human being is precisely the fact that he spoke and acted *without authority* and that he regarded "the exercise of authority" as a pagan characteristic (Mk 10:42 parr)?

Authority means the right to be obeyed by others. To claim authority would mean to claim this right, to claim obedience from others. Mark understood the words of Jesus as indeed words of authority which command obedience and he says as much (1:22, 27). But it is surely significant that the subjects who obey are evil spirits, illnesses, sins, law, winds and seas — not people![10] The English word "authority" is usually reserved for the right to be obeyed by people. The Greek word *exousia* can be extended to cover the power a person has over things too. Luke endeavors to underline this by speaking of *exousia* and *dunamis:* authority and power (9:1).

We have already seen that the power which Jesus had over evil spirits and over evil in general was the power of faith. Jesus' remarkable faith, which healed, cured and saved and which awakened faith in those around him, is being thought of in the gospels as a kind of authority. The analogy is made explicit in the story of that great symbol of authority and obedience, the

Roman centurion. This miracle-story comes from a tradition independent of Mark (Mt 8:5–13; Lk 7:1–10; Jn 4:46–53). In the form in which Matthew and Luke knew it, a comparison is made between the military discipline of unquestioned authority and obedience on the one hand and Jesus' power over evil spirits on the other. The idea is that a person who understands the unfailing effectiveness of military *authority* will appreciate the unfailing effectiveness of Jesus' *faith*, and such a person would have greater faith than anything Jesus had found in Israel, we are told.

The only authority which Jesus can be said to have exercised is a metaphorical or analogous authority, the authority over evil which is the power of faith. But what then of his manner of teaching and preaching?

Nothing could be more unauthoritative than the parables of Jesus. Their whole purpose is to enable listeners to discover something for themselves. They are not illustrations of revealed doctrines; they are works of art which reveal or uncover the truth about life. They awaken faith in listeners so that they can "see" the truth for themselves.[11] That is why Jesus' parables always end with an explicit or implicit question which the listener must answer. "Which of these three do you think proved himself a neighbor?" (Lk 10:36); "Which of them will love him more?" (Lk 7:42); "What is your opinion? Which of the two sons did the father's will?" (Mt 21:28, 31); "Now what will the owner of the vineyard do to them?" (Lk 20:16). The parables of the lost sheep and the lost coin are formulated almost entirely as questions (Lk 15:4–10; Mt 18:12–14).

The parables were addressed not to the poor and the oppressed or to Jesus' disciples but to his opponents.[12] They were intended to persuade and convince. The questions, somewhat like the questions in a Socratic dialogue, have the function of making others think for themselves.

It could be argued that Jesus reasoned in this manner with his opponents who did not accept his authority but when he spoke to his disciples and to the crowds who accepted him as their Teacher he spoke with authority. Most of Jesus' sayings, unlike the parables, are not formulated as questions. They do not appear to be persuasive arguments but authoritative statements of truth.

Yet surely Jesus did not expect only his opponents to think for themselves? Surely his disciples were also expected to judge for themselves (Lk 12:57) and to read the signs of the times for themselves (Lk 12:54–56; Mt 16:2–3)? Would he have expected his disciples to accept whatever he said on "blind" faith?

Jesus wanted others to see what he saw and to believe what he believed. But he had no doubt about the truth of what he saw and believed. He seems to have been extraordinarily confident and sure of himself. It was this that gave the impression of "authority." It was the unparalleled strength of his convictions which made him say (if he did in fact say it at all): "But I say to you . . ." or "Amen, amen I say to you. . . ." Jesus proclaimed the truth without hesitation, whether he was using the persuasive methods of the parable or the more forthright pronouncements of the sayings. There was never any place for "maybe" and "perhaps"; there were no "ifs" and "buts." This is the truth about life; can't you see it?

I can find no evidence that Jesus ever expected his audience to rely upon any authority at all—either his own or that of others. Unlike the scribes, he never appeals to the authority of the rabbinical tradition nor even to the authority of scripture itself. He does not expound the truth by interpreting or commenting upon the sacred text. His perception and teaching of the truth is direct and unmediated. He does not even lay claim to the authority of a prophet, the authority which comes directly from God. Unlike the prophets he does not appeal to a special prophetic calling or to a vision in order to authenticate his words.[13] He never uses the classical prophetic introduction, "God says. . . ." And he refuses to produce any kind of sign from heaven to prove that he can speak in the name of God. In the end, when he is faced directly with the question of what authority he might have, *he refuses to answer the question* (Mk 11:33 parr). People were expected to see the truth of what he was doing and saying without relying upon any authority at all. Linnemann, in her brilliant study of Jesus' parables, concludes that "the only thing that could give weight to the words of Jesus were the words themselves."[14]

Jesus was unique among the people of his time in his ability to overcome all forms of authority-thinking. The only authority which Jesus might be said to have appealed to was the authority of the truth itself. He did not make authority his truth, he made truth his authority. And in so far as the authority of God can be thought of as the authority of truth, Jesus might be said to have appealed to, and to have possessed, the authority of God. But when we speak of the authority of truth (and therefore the authority of God) we are once again using the word "authority" as a metaphor. Jesus did not expect others to obey him; he expected them to "obey" the truth, to live truthfully. Once again it would be better to speak about power here rather than authority. The power of Jesus' words was the power of truth itself. Jesus made a lasting impact upon people because by avoiding all authority-thinking he released the power of truth itself — which is the power of God and indeed the power of faith.

The only thing which Jesus can be said to have claimed is that he spoke the truth. This is a substantial claim, far more substantial than any claim to exalted titles or superhuman authority. What is the basis of this claim? What made Jesus so sure that *his* convictions were infallibly true? One might answer: the convictions themselves. Jesus clearly felt that his insight into reality did not need to be proved or authenticated by anything outside of itself. His insight was an intuitive and self-authenticating *experience.*

This brings us to the very delicate matter of Jesus' personal experience. Any attempt to reconstruct Jesus' psychology or consciousness would be purely conjectural. Most scholars are satisfied with the assertion that somewhere at the heart of Jesus' mysterious personality there was a unique experience of intimate closeness to God — the Abba-experience.[15] This is surely true, all the evidence points in this direction, but is it so impossible to give any account at all of what such an experience might mean?

It is not necessary to speculate about Jesus' psychology. We *know* that he was moved to act and speak by a profound experience of compassion. And we *know* that the Abba-experience was an experience of God as a compassionate Father. This would mean that Jesus experienced the mysterious creative power behind all phenomena (God) as compassion or love. "Everyone who loves is born of God and experiences God; anyone who does not love has never had any experience of God, because God is love" (1 Jn 4:7–8*).

According to Von Rad prophets did not only share God's knowledge, they were also filled to the point of bursting with God's own feelings and emotions.[16] In the case of Jesus it was God's feeling of compassion that possessed him and filled him. All his convictions, his faith and his hope were expressions of this fundamental experience. If God is compassionate, then goodness will triumph over evil, the impossible will happen and there is hope for humankind. Faith and hope are the experience of compassion as a divine emotion.

Compassion is the basis of truth. The experience of compassion is the experience of suffering or feeling with someone. To suffer or feel with humanity, nature and God is to be in tune with the rhythms and impulses of life. This is also the experience of solidarity, solidarity with humanity, nature and God. It excludes every form of alienation and falsehood. It makes a person at one with reality and therefore true and authentic in himself.

The secret of Jesus' infallible insight and unshakable convictions was his unfailing experience of solidarity with God, which revealed itself as an experience of solidarity with humanity and nature. This made of him a uniquely liberated man, uniquely courageous, fearless, independent, hopeful and truthful.

What would make anyone want to destroy such a man? What would make anyone want to arrest him and try him?

# Chapter 18

# ON TRIAL

The events that led up to Jesus' death and the motives that were at work are puzzling and confusing. One gets the impression that the people involved were themselves muddled and confused.

In order to bring some measure of clarity into the picture for ourselves we need to distinguish between the charges which they could have brought against Jesus, the charges which they actually did bring against him and the real motives for wanting to destroy him. The gospels themselves witness to this threefold distinction: for example, Jesus could have been charged with deliberately breaking the Sabbath or practicing magic (casting out devils by the power of Satan); he was actually charged with claiming to be the Messiah-king; and the real motive, according to Mark followed by Matthew, was envy or jealousy (Mk 15:10; Mt 27:18). Unfortunately the aims of the gospel-writers did not compel them to maintain this distinction throughout. Charges which could have been brought against him were sometimes treated as charges that were in fact brought against him (e.g., blasphemy, Mk 14:64 par) and charges which were in fact brought against him were sometimes treated as the real motives for rejecting him (e.g., that he claimed to be the Messiah, Mk 14:62–64). This has led to a great deal of confusion.

Secondly we must distinguish between the part played by the Jewish leaders and the part played by the Roman government.

There were two courts or tribunals: the Sanhedrin or Jewish court, which consisted of the high priest and some seventy chief priests, elders and scribes; and the Roman court, which was presided over by Pilate as the procurator or governor. Jesus was tried, sentenced and executed by the Roman court. But the gospel-writers, like all early Christians, endeavored to make it quite clear that, in spite of this, the Jewish leaders were more to blame for Jesus' death than the Romans. They were absolutely right but the manner in which they set about demonstrating this to their readers has led to endless confusion — especially when they give the impression that the interrogation by the Jewish leaders was a kind of trial.[1]

Their intention was not to deceive or to twist the historical facts. Their intention was to help the reader to understand what really happened despite all appearances. On the surface of it the Romans were to blame but the truth of the matter was that the Jews were more guilty. There is no anti-semitism here, nor is there a prejudice in favor of Rome, only disappointment. The truth of the matter is that Jesus appealed to a particular nation at a particular time and that nation rejected him as most other people might well have done in the circumstances.

What *did* happen?

The charge upon which Jesus was tried, sentenced and executed was that he claimed to be the Messiah or king of the Jews. That was all that Pilate asked him about and that was all that appeared on his cross as the charge against him. Everything else is mere speculation: what he could have been charged for or accused of. The Sanhedrin could have charged him with being a false teacher or a false prophet or a rebellious son (Dt 21:20–21) or of deliberately breaking the sabbath or of practicing magic.[2] The early Christians thought that some Jews had accused Jesus of *blasphemy* because he had forgiven sins (Mk 2:7 parr) and because he had claimed to be the Messiah, Son of God or "son of man" (Mk 14:61–64 par), which was tantamount to making himself equal to God (Jn 5:18; 10:33, 36; 19:7). They also thought that this could have been the charge brought against him before the Sanhedrin (Mk 14:61–64 par) or that this could have been the reason why the people asked Pilate to crucify him (Jn 19:7).

According to Luke, the Jews accused him of, and the Romans could have charged him with, subversive activity and opposing the payment of taxes to Caesar (23:2). There was a sense in which his activity and his teaching were subversive of the *status quo*. He wanted to change society from top to bottom. About the issue of taxation, as we have seen, he carefully avoided coming down in favor of either side in the controversy because for him it was not the real issue.

What all this means is that, although there were several possible charges or accusations that could have been brought against him, the Sanhedrin did not try him at all and the Romans tried him for claiming to be the king of the Jews. Why? What were their real motives for doing this?

Pilate was a particularly ruthless governor. He went out of his way to provoke the Jews and when they protested or rebelled he did not scruple to surround them and slaughter them. Alleged rebels were very often executed without a trial at all. According to Philo,[3] the contemporary Jewish philosopher, Pilate was "by nature inflexible, self-willed and hard." He lists Pilate's crimes as "bribery, tyranny, pillage, violence, calumny, constant execution without passing a verdict, and endless, insufferable cruelty."

This picture is confirmed by the three incidents during the administration of Pilate which were recorded by the contemporary Jewish historian, Josephus. The first incident concerned the Roman standards or imperial insignia, which the Jews regarded as idolatrous because they bore images of the emperor and other sacred symbols. Despite the fact that it had not been done before, Pilate ordered the standards to be taken to Jerusalem. The people protested and petitioned Pilate to remove the standards. Pilate refused, had them secretly surrounded and would have had them slaughtered but for the fact that they put up no resistance and were all willing to die as martyrs.[4] It would not have been politically expedient to kill them all in cold blood. However, during the second clash between Pilate and the Jewish crowd, this time about his use of Temple funds to build an aqueduct, he had them surrounded and battered with clubs. Some were killed and others seriously hurt.[5] The third incident led to his downfall. He was sent back to Rome on account of it.

This time it concerned a group of Samaritans who had gathered on Mount Gerizim for the innocent enough purpose of searching for the sacred vessels which they believed Moses had hidden there. Pilate sent his army out to slaughter them.[6]

Pilate seems to have had a phobia about large gatherings of people. Whenever the Jews (or Samaritans) gathered to make common cause about something, he suspected a potential rebellion against Rome.

We get exactly the same picture of Pilate from the brief mention of another incident in the New Testament itself. Luke speaks of "the Galilean whose blood Pilate had mingled with that of their sacrifices" (13:1)—a massacre in the Temple!

This, of course, is not the picture of Pilate we find in the gospel accounts of Jesus' *trial*. It is obvious that Pilate is being somewhat whitewashed in these accounts of the trial in order to make the more important point that the Jews were to blame for Jesus' death.

What would Pilate in fact have thought of Jesus?

We know what other, less ruthless, procurators thought of prophets and potential Messiahs. In about 45 C.E. a prophet called Theudas led a large number of Jews with their belongings down to the Jordan River, which, like Moses, he promised to divide miraculously so they could cross over into the desert. The procurator, Cuspius Fadus, dispatched his cavalry. They killed some and took others prisoner. Theudas was beheaded.[7] There is no evidence that Theudas was a Zealot.[8]

The incident of the Jewish prophet from Egypt may also be cited here. In about 58 C.E. he assembled a crowd of people on the Mount of Olives promising, like Joshua, that the city walls would fall at his command. The procurator, Antonius Felix, took action immediately. Many Jews were killed but the Egyptian escaped.[9] Later a Roman officer mistook Paul for the Egyptian Jew, who he says was the leader of the four thousand Sicarii or cut-throats (Acts 21:38). They were not Zealots although their prophet-leader may have had intentions which were very similar to those of the Zealots.

If Pilate had known Jesus' intentions, if he had known what kind of "kingdom" Jesus was hoping for and how much Jesus was trying to spread faith in this "kingdom," he would certainly have wanted to destroy him. Pilate would have regarded Jesus as a very serious political threat even if he had known that Jesus did not intend setting up the new "kingdom" by force of arms – just as Herod had regarded John the Baptist as a political threat and thought it necessary to have him arrested, even though John had never resorted to violence.[10] Armed rebellion was not the only threat to Roman rule. Any popular movement that was intent upon change, especially if it was religiously motivated, would have been regarded as extremely dangerous.

But this is what Pilate would have thought *if* he had known Jesus' teaching and intentions. Did Pilate in fact know anything about Jesus?

He may well have known about the incident in the Temple courtyard when Jesus expelled the traders. The Roman garrison overlooked the Temple courtyard and when Paul caused a riot outside the Temple gates the Roman soldiers soon intervened (Acts 21:27–36). The "cleansing" of the Temple courtyard by Jesus could not possibly have gone unnoticed. This alone would have been enough to make Pilate suspicious of Jesus and his intentions. But we cannot be sure whether the Roman garrison reported the matter to Pilate or not.

At the time of Jesus' trial Pilate knew, at the very least, that Jesus was an influential leader and that many of his followers regarded him as the future Messiah or king of the Jews.[11] But did Pilate know this before the trial? It seems as if he must have known.

We learn from John that Jesus was arrested by a mixed group of Jewish guards and *Roman soldiers* ( 18:3, 12). In view of John's tendency to play down Roman guilt wherever he could, this inclusion of Roman soldiers and their captain (18:12) must be an historical fact. No Jew, not even the high priest, could have commissioned Roman soldiers to arrest someone. Pilate must have been in on it. Pilate must have wanted Jesus arrested. He must therefore have known about Jesus *before* the trial.

We can conclude that, had Pilate not become suspicious of Jesus and his intentions on the occasion of the Temple incident, he must have found out about Jesus some time after this but before the arrest.

What part, then, did the Jewish authorities have in this affair?

The high priest was appointed by the Romans. He was allowed to exercise authority and to share in the administration of the country. Even his religious functions were controlled by the Romans, who had his sacred vestments in their keeping. The high priest and his associates were therefore deeply involved in what we would call politics or affairs of state, and totally dependent upon the Romans. Their task was to help maintain peace, especially during the overcrowded festivals in Jerusalem.

How much did *they* know about Jesus? Probably very little. They must have known at least as much as Pilate did but not enough to bring against him the charges which could have been brought against him according to Jewish law (presuming that they ever did consider bringing him to a trial by the Sanhedrin). We can feel sure they knew that Jesus was inciting the people to believe in the imminent arrival of the "kingdom" of God and that some of the people saw in him the promised Messiah.[12] Such propaganda would have been regarded by the high priest and his associates as, in the very first place, a threat to the delicate maintenance of peace with the Romans. They were men of affairs, more concerned about expediency than truth.

This is clear from their deliberations about Jesus some time before his arrest. It is John again who gives us an account of these deliberations.

> "What are we going to do ... ? If we let him go on in this way everybody will believe in him and the Romans will come and take our place and our nation." Caiaphas, the high priest that year, said, "... it is more expedient for one man to die ... than for the whole nation to be destroyed." (11:47–50*)

There is no concern here for the truth and especially not for what many today would call religious truth. It is a matter of political expediency. What will the Roman reprisals be if we do not do something about this man? Would it not be more expedient for him to die?

There are only two possible ways of making sense of these deliberations. The one is that Caiaphas was of the opinion that the propaganda about a new "kingdom" and the popular acclaim of Jesus as the Messiah-king were about to precipitate a clash between Jesus and the Romans. If this happened the Romans would "come and take our place and our nation." Paul Winter has argued that "our place" does not mean the Holy Place or Temple but the position or status of the high priest and his council.[13] If this is so, then Caiaphas's fear was that they would all be deprived of their positions because they had neglected their duty in not preventing an uprising by reporting the matter to the Romans or handing Jesus over to them for execution.

The other possibility is that Pilate had already ordered them to find Jesus and hand him over. The deliberations of the Jewish authorities would then have been about a case of extradition. Should a Jew whose extradition on a political charge was demanded by a pagan overlord be handed over or not? The maxim that "it is more expedient for one man to die than for the whole nation to be destroyed" sounds very much like the controversial legal maxim that the wanted man should be handed over "lest the entire community suffer on his account."[14]

In other words what we have here is either a preventive measure calculated to avoid a clash with the Romans or a case of extradition. In either case the decision of the high priest and his council was *to collaborate with Rome.* Political expediency demanded that this man be handed over and allowed to die. To attempt to save his life would be national suicide.

It was the Romans, then, who wanted to destroy Jesus. Whether they had found out about Jesus themselves and wanted an extradition, or whether they were told about him by Caiaphas after the deliberations of the council, remains uncertain. That they should have wanted to destroy Jesus is fully in accord with the known policy of Pilate and other procurators. They destroyed all prophets and potential Messiahs.

The Jewish authorities, for whatever reasons, decided to find Jesus and hand him over to Pilate. The accusation which we must make against them is that they *betrayed* Jesus. To hand over and to betray are the same word in Greek: *paradidomai* (Mk 9:31 parr; 10:33, 34 parr; 14:41 par; 15:1 par; Mt 26:2; Jn 19:11; Acts 7:52). There were therefore two betrayals: Judas betrayed him (handed him over) to the Jewish authorities and they in turn betrayed him (handed him over) to the Romans

(Mk 10:33–34 parr). He was then tried and sentenced to death by a Roman court.

The most remarkable thing about the trial itself, the one thing about which we can be absolutely certain and yet the one thing that is frequently overlooked, is that *Jesus did not defend himself.* Throughout all the proceedings, no matter who accused him or what they accused him of, Jesus remained *silent* (Mk 14:60–61; 15:4–5; Mt 26:62–63; 27:12, 14; Lk 23:9). If and when he did speak, it was only in order to be non-committal and in effect to refuse to give an answer: "It is you who say it" (Mk 15:2; Mt 26:64; 27:11; Lk 22:70; 23:3) and "If I tell you, you will not believe me and if I question you, you will not answer" (Lk 22:67; see also 20:8; Jn 18:20–21). The dialogue, which was constructed by the gospel writers or their sources in order to give expression to the relationship between Jesus and his opponents, should not obscure their own plain statement of the facts: "He offered no reply to any of the charges" (Mt 27:14).

The suffering servant in Isaiah 53:7 was silent before his accusers—like a lamb before its shearers. It cannot be argued from this that the gospel writers or their sources invented the idea of Jesus' silence in order to point out that Jesus was the suffering servant.[15] Remaining silent before his accusers is exactly what we might have expected Jesus to do. He had consistently refused to produce signs from heaven; he had never argued from authority; he had refused to answer questions about his own authority; and now he refused to defend or justify his behavior.

In other words, Jesus stood there without a word, putting everyone else to the test. The truth of the matter is that it was not Jesus who was on trial. His betrayers and accusers were on trial before him. His silence puzzled, disturbed, questioned and tested them. Their words were turned back at them and they condemned themselves out of their own mouths.

Pilate, firstly, was tried and found wanting. Jesus' silence took him by surprise (Mt 27:14 par). He probably did hesitate for a moment, as all the gospel accounts suggest. But because he was not, and had never been, concerned about the truth, he went on to do what political expediency seemed to demand. As John saw so clearly, Pilate was guilty of a lack of interest in the truth (18:37–38).

Caiaphas and his associates were still more guilty. It must have been very difficult to decide between the life of one man and the future of the nation. But even more so than Pilate, Caiaphas and his associates could have gone to the trouble of finding out more about Jesus and they could have been open to the possibility that he had something worthwhile to offer.

But even if Caiaphas had been open to the truth and had come to believe Jesus, what could he or should he have done in order to secure peace with the Romans? Perhaps, we can say, he should have risked his own life by resigning as high priest, joining Jesus in hiding and working with him to spread faith in the "kingdom." This is a tall order and one wonders how many men in his position would ever have been so concerned about truth and honesty. And yet was it not for this very reason that the men of that time were on the brink of disaster? Caiaphas was not able to measure up to the challenge with which Jesus presented him. Which one of us would want to throw the first stone at Caiaphas?

The death of Jesus was also a judgment upon the scribes, Pharisees and others who knowingly rejected him. If they had accepted him and believed in the "kingdom" of the poor, that "kingdom" would have come instead of the catastrophe. They were no different from so many men and women today and yet in the trial of Jesus they too were found guilty.

Finally the disciples themselves were being put to the test. It was a severe test, a test of their willingness to die with him for the sake of humankind. But Judas betrayed him, Peter denied him and the rest fled.

Jesus himself was also tried and tested. He sweated blood over it and told his disciples to pray that they would not have to be as severely tested as he was (Mk 14:32–38 parr). He had always taught his disciples to hope and pray that it would not come to this, that God would not bring them to the test or trial. That is the meaning of the prayer: "Lead us not into temptation" (Mt 6:13; Lk 11:4).[16] Jesus did not want anyone to be put to the test.

But the crisis came and the test was severe. Jesus alone was able to accept the challenge of the hour. It set him above everyone else as the silent truth that judges every human being. Jesus died alone as the only person who had been able to survive the test.[17] Everyone else failed and yet everyone else was given another chance. The history of Christianity is the history of those who came to believe in Jesus and who were inspired to take up the challenge of his death—in one way or another.

## Chapter 19

# FAITH IN JESUS

Jesus did not found an organization; he inspired a movement. It was inevitable that the movement would quite soon become an organization but in the beginning there were simply people, scattered individuals and groups, who had been inspired by Jesus. There were the twelve, the women, his family (Mary, James, Jude), many of the poor and the oppressed who had been put on their feet by him; there were disciples in Galilee and disciples in Jericho (e.g., Zacchaeus) and Jerusalem (e.g., Joseph of Arimathaea and Nicodemus); there were Greek-speaking Jews like the seven Hellenists who were inspired by what they had heard about him (Acts 6:1–6); there were even Pharisees and priests who joined the community that had been formed in Jerusalem (Acts 6:7; 15:5).

Each remembered Jesus in his or her own way or had been struck by a particular aspect of what they had heard about him. There were at first no doctrines and no dogmas, no universally accepted way of following him or believing in him.

Jesus had no successor. He had not inspired the kind of movement which simply goes on by appointing successors to the original leader. The Zealots, like the Maccabees before them, had a dynastic or hereditary succession. But the remarkable thing about the movement inspired by Jesus was that he himself remained the leader and the inspiration of his followers even after his death. Jesus was obviously felt to be irreplaceable. If he died, the movement died. But if the movement continued to live, then it could only be because in some sense or another Jesus continued to live.

The movement was pluriform, indeed amorphous and haphazard. Its only unity or point of cohesion was the personality of Jesus himself. Not that this was ever, as far as we know, a matter of merely perpetuating his teaching or his memory. The early Christians were those who continued to experience or began to experience, in one way or another, the power of Jesus' presence among them after his death. Everyone felt that despite his death Jesus was still leading, guiding and inspiring them. Some of those who had known him and seen him before he died (especially the twelve) were convinced that they had seen him alive again after his death and that he had instructed them again as he had done before. The women who discovered the empty tomb, followed by the other disciples, proclaimed that Jesus had risen from the dead.

Many also experienced the continued leadership and inspiration of Jesus as the inheriting of his Spirit—the Spirit of God. They felt that they were possessed by his Spirit and were being led by his Spirit. The prophecy of Joel was being fulfilled in them through Jesus: the Spirit had been poured out among them, making them all prophets who see visions and dream dreams (see Peter's sermon in Acts 2:14–41). Jesus remained present and active through the presence and activity of his Spirit: "Now this Lord is the Spirit, and where the Spirit of the Lord is, there is freedom . . . this is the work of the Lord who is Spirit" (2 Cor 4:17–18).

Jesus had made and continued to make such a profound impact upon his followers that they found it impossible to believe that anyone could be equal to him or greater—not even Moses or Elijah (Mk 9:2–8 parr), not even Abraham (Jn 8:58). That a prophet or judge or Messiah should come after Jesus and be greater than Jesus was inconceivable (Jn 7:31). It was not necessary "to wait for someone else" (Mt 11:3 par). Jesus was everything. Jesus was everything that the Jews had ever hoped and prayed for. Jesus had fulfilled or was about to fulfill every promise and every prophecy. If anyone is to judge the world in the end it must be he (Acts 10:42; 17:31). If anyone is to be appointed Messiah, King, Lord, Son of God in the "kingdom," how could it be anyone but Jesus (Acts 2:36; 3:20–21; Rom 1:4; Rev 17:14; 19:16)?

Their admiration and veneration for him knew no bounds. He was in every way the ultimate, the only criterion of good and evil and of truth and falsehood, the only hope for the future, the only power which could transform the world. Jesus' followers exalted him to the right hand of God, or rather they believed that in God's estimation Jesus was at God's right hand (Acts 2:33–34; 5:31; Eph 1:20–23; 1 Cor 15:24–27; 1 Pet 3:21–22; Heb 10:12–13). God contradicts the assessment of the Jewish leaders. They rejected Jesus, betrayed him and had him killed but God raises him up, glorifies him, exalts him and makes him the Lord, the Messiah, the cornerstone (Acts 2:22, 36; 3:13–15; 4:11; 5:30–31; 1 Pet 2:4).

Jesus was experienced as *the* breakthrough in the history of humanity. He transcended everything that had ever been said and done before. He was in every way the ultimate, the last word. He was on a par with God. His word was God's word. His Spirit was God's Spirit. His feelings were God's feelings. What he stood for was exactly the same as what God stood for. No higher estimation was conceivable.

To believe in Jesus today is to agree with this assessment of him. We do not need to use the same words, the same concepts or the same titles. We do not need to use titles at all. But if we relegate Jesus and what he stands for to second place in our scale of values, then we have already denied him and what he stands for. What Jesus was concerned with was a matter of life and death, a matter of ultimate importance. Either you accept the "kingdom" as Jesus understood it or you don't. You cannot serve two "masters." It is all or nothing. Second place or half measures are tantamount to nothing. To believe in Jesus is to believe that he is divine.

Everyone has a god—in the sense that everyone puts something first in one's life: money, power, prestige, self, career, love and so forth. There must be something in your life which operates as your source of meaning and strength, something which you regard, at least implicitly, as the supreme power in your life. If you think your priority in life is to be a transcendent person, you will have a God with a capital letter. If you think of your highest value as a cause, an ideal or an ideology, you will have a god with a small letter. Either way you will have something that is divine for you.

To believe that Jesus is divine is to choose to make him and what he stands for your God. To deny this is to make someone else your god or God, and to relegate Jesus and what he stands for to second place in your scale of values.

I have chosen this approach because it enables us to begin with an open concept of divinity and to avoid the perennial mistake of superimposing upon the life and personality of Jesus our preconceived ideas about what God is supposed to be like. The traditional image of God has become so difficult to understand and so difficult to reconcile with the historical facts of Jesus' life that many people are no longer able to identify Jesus with *that* God. For many young people today Jesus is very much alive but the traditional God is dead.[1]

By his words and his praxis, Jesus himself changed the content of the word "God." If we do not allow him to change our image of God, we will not be able to say that *he* is our Lord and our God. To choose him as our God is to make him the source of our information about divinity and to refuse to superimpose upon him our own ideas of divinity.

This is the meaning of the traditional assertion that Jesus is the Word of God. Jesus reveals God to us, God does not reveal Jesus to us. God is not the Word of Jesus, that is to say, our ideas about God cannot throw any light upon the life of Jesus. To argue from God to Jesus instead of arguing from Jesus to God is to put the cart before the horse. This, of course, is what many Christians have tried to do. It has generally led them into a series of meaningless speculations which only cloud the issue and which prevent Jesus from revealing God to us.

We cannot deduce anything about Jesus from what we think we know about God; we must now deduce everything about God from what we do know about Jesus. Thus, when we say that Jesus is divine, we do not wish to *add* anything to what we have been able to discover about him so far, nor do we wish to *change* anything that we have said about him. To say now suddenly that Jesus is divine does not change our understanding of Jesus; it changes our understanding of divinity. We are not only turning away from the gods of money, power, prestige or self; we are turning away from all the old images of a personal God in order to find our God in Jesus and what he stood for.

This is not to say that we must abolish the Old Testament and reject the God of Abraham, Isaac and Jacob. It means that if we accept Jesus as divine, we must reinterpret the Old Testament from Jesus' point of view and we must try to understand the God of Abraham, Isaac and Jacob in the way in which Jesus did. We accept the God of the Old Testament as one who has now changed and relented of God's former purposes in order to be totally compassionate toward humankind — all humankind.

To accept Jesus as our God is to accept the one whom Jesus called *Abba* as our God. This supreme power, this power of goodness, truth and love which is stronger than any other power in the world, can now be seen and recognized in Jesus — *both* in what he had to say about *Abba and* in what he himself was, the very structure of his personal life and the almighty power of his convictions. Our God is both Jesus and *Abba*. Because of their essential unity or "exact sameness," when we worship the one we worship the other. And yet they are distinguishable in that Jesus alone is visible to us, Jesus alone is our source of information about divinity, Jesus alone is the Word of God.

We have seen what Jesus was like. If we now wish to treat him as our God, we would have to conclude that our God does not want to be served by us, but wants to serve us; God does not want to be given the highest possible rank and status in our society, but wants to take the lowest place and to be without any rank and status; God does not want to be feared and obeyed, but wants to be recognized in the sufferings of the poor and the weak; God is not supremely indifferent and detached, but is irrevocably committed to the liberation of humankind, for God has chosen to be identified with all people in a spirit of solidarity and compassion. If this is not a true picture of God, then Jesus is not divine. If this is a true picture of God, then God is more truly human, more thoroughly humane, than any human being. God is, what Schillebeeckx has called, a *Deus humanissimus*, a supremely human God.[2]

Whatever humanity and divinity may mean in terms of a static philosophy of metaphysical natures, in religious terms for the people who recognize Jesus as their God, the human and the divine have been brought together in such a way that they now represent one and the same religious value. In this sense Jesus' divinity is not something totally different from his humanity, something we have to add to his humanity; Jesus' divinity is the transcendent depths of his humanity. Jesus was immeasurably more human than other human beings, and that is what we value above all other things when we recognize him as divine, when we acknowledge him as our Lord and our God.

But are there any objective and historical grounds for believing that this man, as a human being, is divine? To choose something like money or power as one's god is purely subjective and arbitrary—a form of idolatry. To choose Jesus need not be purely subjective and arbitrary because, in this case, it is possible to give a reasonable and convincing account of one's choice.

There are ways of accounting for our faith in Jesus' divinity which are hopelessly unsatisfactory. Many Christians argue that Jesus himself claimed to be divine, either explicitly by claiming divine titles or divine authority, or implicitly by speaking and acting with divine authority. These claims are then sometimes said to have been "proved" or confirmed by his miracles and/or his resurrection.

As we have seen, Jesus did not claim divine titles or divine authority, but he did claim to know the truth and to know it without having to rely upon any authority other than the truth itself. He claimed, at least by implication, that he was in immediate contact with the truth, or rather that in him the truth itself was finding expression. Thus, as we have seen, his audience was not expected to rely blindly upon his authority, but to catch from him the truth which he was and spoke, the truth which he had not received from anyone else. By learning from him they were in fact making the truth itself their authority. Those who were convinced by Jesus were convinced by the persuasiveness of the truth itself. Jesus was uniquely in harmony with all that is true and real in life. His spontaneous compassion for people precluded any kind of alienation or artificiality. His spontaneous faith in the power of goodness and truth is indicative of a life without falsehood and illusion. One could say that he was absorbed by the truth, or, better still, that in him the truth became flesh.

Jesus himself would have experienced this as being in complete harmony with God. He must have been aware of the fact that he was thinking and feeling as God thinks and feels. He therefore felt no need to refer to, or rely upon, any authority or any power outside of his own experience.

But how are we to know whether this claim to truthfulness was an illusion or not? There is no scientific or historical way of proving it or disproving it. Like the proverbial tree, it can only be tested by its fruits. If the fruits, Jesus' sayings and doings, ring true for us, then the experience upon which they were based could not have been an illusion. Once we have listened to Jesus with an open mind, and once we have been persuaded and convinced by what he has to say about life, we will know that his claim to first-hand experience of the truth was no hollow boast. As soon as Jesus has been able to awaken in us a faith in what he stood for, we shall respond by putting our faith in him and making his unique truthfulness our God. In other words, *the faith which Jesus awakens in us is at the same time faith in him and faith in his divinity.*

This was the experience of Jesus' followers. This was the kind of impact he had upon them. They would not have articulated it in this way; but then it is, after all, not a matter of theories about Jesus or the Godhead. Words and theories will always be inadequate. In the last analysis faith is not a way of speaking or a way of thinking, it is a way of living and can only be adequately articulated in a living praxis. To acknowledge Jesus as our Lord and Savior is only meaningful in so far as we try to live as he lived and to order our lives according to his values. We do not need to theorize about Jesus, we need to "re-produce" him in our time and our circumstances. He himself did not regard the truth as something we simply "uphold" and "maintain," but as something we choose to live and experience. So that our search, like his search, is primarily a search for *orthopraxis* (true practice) rather than *orthodoxy* (true doctrine).[3] Only a true practice of the faith can verify what we believe. We can refer to traditional authorities and theological arguments, but what we believe can only be made true, and be seen to be true, in the concrete results which faith achieves in the world—today and tomorrow.[4]

The beginning of faith in Jesus, then, is the attempt to read the signs of our times as Jesus read the signs of his times. There are similarities but there are also differences. We cannot merely repeat what Jesus said; but we can begin to analyze our times in the same spirit as he analyzed his times.

We would have to begin, as Jesus did, with compassion—compassion for the starving millions, for those who are humiliated and rejected, and for the billions of the future who will suffer because of the way we live today. It is only when, like the good Samaritan, we discover our common humanity, that we shall begin to experience what Jesus experienced. Only those who value above all else the dignity of human beings as human beings are in agreement with the God who created humanity in God's own image and likeness and who is "no respecter of persons" (Acts 10:34 AV). As Paul Verghese of the Syrian Orthodox Church in Kerala has put it: "It is not the Christian Gospel which undermines man in order to exalt God. It is too petty a God who can have glory only at the expense of the glory of man."[5] Faith in Jesus without respect and compassion for people is a lie (compare 1 Cor 13:1–2; James 2:14–26). To identify with Jesus is to identify with all people.

Searching for the signs of the times in the spirit of Jesus, then, will mean recognizing all the forces that are working against humanity as the forces of evil. Is the present world order not ruled and governed by Satan, the enemy of humanity? Is the system not the modern equivalent of the "kingdom" of Satan? Are the powers of evil not dragging us all along to our destruction, to a hell on earth? We shall have to try to understand the structures of evil in the world as it is today. How much have we been basing ourselves upon the worldly values of money, possessions, prestige, status, privilege, power and upon the group solidarities of family, race, class, party, religion and nationalism? To make these our supreme values is to have nothing in common with Jesus.

To believe in Jesus is to believe that goodness can and will triumph over evil. Despite the system, despite the magnitude, complexity and apparent insolubility of our problems today, humanity can be, and in the end will be, liberated. Every form of evil — sin and all the consequences of sin: sickness, suffering, misery, frustration, fear, oppression and injustice — can be overcome. And the only power that can achieve this is the power of a faith that believes this. For faith is, as we have seen, the power of goodness and truth, the power of God.

There is a power that can resist the system and prevent it from destroying us. There is a motive that can replace, and can be stronger than, the profit motive. There is an incentive that can mobilize the world, enable the "haves" to lower their standard of living and make us only too willing to redistribute the world's wealth and its population. It is the same drive and incentive that motivated Jesus: *compassion* and *faith*. It has generally been called faith, hope and love; whatever you choose to call it, you must understand it as the unleashing of the divine but thoroughly "natural" power of truth, goodness and beauty.

With this kind of approach to the problems of our time one will surely come to recognize the impending catastrophe as a unique opportunity for the coming of the "kingdom." For us the impending catastrophe is total and definitive. It is the event which defines our time; it is our *eschaton*. But if we allow it to shake the very foundations of our life, we may find that Jesus has awakened in us the faith and the hope to see the signs of the "kingdom" here in our midst, to see our *eschaton* as an either-or event and to see our time as the unique opportunity for the total liberation of humankind. God is speaking to us in a new way today. God is speaking to us in the events and problems of our time. Jesus can help us to understand the voice of Truth but, in the last analysis, it is we who must decide and act.

# NOTES

## 1. A NEW PERSPECTIVE

1. Edward Schillebeeckx, *God, the Future of Man*, p. 24.

2. Recent statistics on these issues are available in many sources, including Sean McDonagh, *The Greening of the Church*, Maryknoll, NY: Orbis Books and London: Geoffrey Chapman, 1990 and Paul Vallely, *Bad Samaritans: First World Ethics and Third World Debt*, Maryknoll, NY: Orbis Books and London: Hodder & Stoughton, 1990.

3. Rubem Alves calls it the "organization" or the "dinosaur": *Tomorrow's Child*, pp. 1–22.

4. Alves, pp. 34–36.

5. *The State of the World's Children: 1990 Report*, UNICEF, as quoted in Vallely, *Bad Samaritans*, p. 3.

6. *Spiral of Violence*, London, 1971, p. 30.

## 2. THE PROPHECY OF JOHN THE BAPTIST

1. For a convenient summary of what scholars regard as historically certain about Jesus, see Leslie E. Mitton, *Jesus: The Fact behind the Faith*. See also John Dominic Crossan, *The Historical Jesus: The Life of a Mediterranean Jewish Peasant*, San Francisco: HarperSan Francisco, 1991 and John P. Meier, *A Marginal Jew: Rethinking the Historical Jesus*, New York: Doubleday, 1991.

2. James M. Robinson, *A New Quest of the Historical Jesus*, pp. 67f, 105; Leonardo Boff, "Salvation of Jesus Christ and the Process of Liberation," *Concilium*, June 1974, pp. 79–80.

3. Josephus, *History of the Jewish War against the Romans*, 2:118 and *The Antiquities of the Jews*, 18:1–10.

4. Josephus, *Jewish War*, 2:254–257; cf. S. G. F. Brandon, *Jesus and the Zealots*, pp. 39–40.

5. Brandon, pp. 37, 47, 54.

6. Josephus, *Antiquities*, 17:2.

7. Joachim Jeremias, *Jerusalem in the Time of Jesus*, p. 246.

8. 1QM 1, 15–19, cf. G. Vermes, *The Dead Sea Scrolls in English*, pp. 123, 125, 143–148.

9. Despite Philo (*Quod omnis probus liber sit*, 78), whose account of the Essenes is not reliable, cf. Edmund Sutcliffe, *The Monks of Qumran*, Westminster, MD: Newman Press, 1960; London, 1960, p. 125.

10. Brandon, p. 61.

11. J. Le Moyne, *Les Sadducéens*, p. 378.

12. Le Moyne, pp. 349–350.

13. Jeremias, pp. 222–232.

14. D. S. Russell, *The Method and Message of Jewish Apocalyptic*, chapter 4.

15. Edmund Schillebeeckx, *Jesus: An Experiment in Christology*, p. 129.

16. Jeremias, *New Testament Theology*, pp. 80–82, Charles H. H. Scobie, *John the Baptist*, pp. 118–120.

17. Schillebeeckx, p. 130.

18. Lloyd Gaston, *No Stone on Another*, p. 138.

19. Schillebeeckx, p. 134; Gaston, p. 138.

20. Gerhard von Rad, *The Message of the Prophets*, pp. 98–99; Russell, pp. 274–275.

21. *Antiquities*, 18:116–119.

22. Scobie, p. 183.

23. "The Fall of Jerusalem and the 'Abomination of Desolation,' " *Journal of Roman Studies*, 37 (1947), 47–54.

24. See note 18 above.

### 3. THE POOR AND THE OPPRESSED

1. E.g., Mk 1:23, 32–34, 40; 2:3, 15, 17; 3:1; 9:17–18, 42; 12:40, 42; Lk 4:18; 5:27; 6:20–21; 7:34, 37, 39; 10:21; 11:46; 14:13, 21; 15:1–2; 18:10, 13, 22; Mt 5:10–12; 8:28; 9:10, 14; 10:3, 15, 42; 11:28; 15:24; 19:30; 20:16; 21:31–32; 25:40, 45; Jn 7:49; 9:1–2, 8, 34.

2. Joachim Jeremias, *New Testament Theology*, p. 112.

3. Johann B. Metz, "The Future in the Memory of Suffering," *Concilium*, June 1972, p. 16; Alves, pp. 129–130.

4. J. Duncan M. Derrett, *Jesus's Audience*, pp. 40, 42.

5. Derrett, pp. 53–55.

6. Jeremias, pp. 112–113.

7. Jeremias maintains that we should call these people toll collec-

tors or tax gatherers or publicans rather than tax collectors in order to distinguish between the hired gatherers who were hated and the state officials whom one never encountered. Jeremias, p. 110; *Jerusalem in the Time of Jesus*, p. 228.

8. Aboth 1:5.

9. Derrett, pp. 117–118.

10. Derrett, p. 63.

11. Derrett, p. 122.

12. Jeremias, *New Testament Theology*, p. 93.

13. Jeremias, *New Testament Theology*, p. 92; *The Eucharistic Words of Jesus.*

14. Dt. 23:3. See Jeremias, *Jerusalem in the Time of Jesus*, pp. 337–342.

15. Jeremias, pp. 275–276, 297–298, 337.

16. Derrett, p. 122.

17. Jeremias, *New Testament Theology*, p. 110, where he says this of tax collectors (or rather toll collectors) but it applies to all the oppressed.

18. Jeremias, *Jerusalem in the Time of Jesus*, p. 297.

19. Was this why in 66 C.E. they burned the Jerusalem archives, which contained the record of their debts? See Josephus, *The Wars of the Jews*, 2:427.

20. Jeremias, pp. 147–232.

21. Jn 7:41, 45–52, cf. Geza Vermes, *Jesus the Jew*, pp. 42–57.

## 4. HEALING

1. Geza Vermes, *Jesus the Jew*, p. 64.

2. Vermes, pp. 69–78.

3. Vermes, pp. 64–65.

4. Vermes, p. 76.

5. Mk 5:34 parr; 10:52 par; Mt 9:28–29; Lk 17:19; and see also Mk 5:36 par; 8:13; 15:28.

6. Gerhard Ebeling, *Word and Faith*, pp. 232–233.

7. Ebeling, pp. 227–232.

8. Cf. Joachim Jeremias, *New Testament Theology*, p. 92.

9. Jürgen Moltmann, *Theology of Hope.*

10. Cf. Reginald H. Fuller, *Interpreting the Miracles*, pp. 8–11.

11. Cf. Emmanuel M. Papper, "Acupuncture: Medicine or Magic?" in *Encyclopedia Britannica Yearbook of Science and the Future*, 1974, pp. 55–56.

12. See, for example, *The Jerome Biblical Commentary*, 3:29.

13. Etienne Trocmé, *Jesus as Seen by His Contemporaries*, pp. 103–105.

14. Jeremias, p. 89.

15. Jeremias, pp. 86–88.

## 5. FORGIVENESS

1. Geza Vermes, *Jesus the Jew*, pp. 72–78.

2. Cf. Edward Schillebeeckx, *Jesus: An Experiment in Christology*, p. 95.

3. The Greek word here *prosdechetai* is best translated "he entertains." See Eta Linnemann, *Jesus of the Parables*, p. 69.

4. E. Lohmeyer, *Das Evangelium des Markus*, Göttingen 1967, p. 55; Joachim Jeremias, *New Testament Theology*, p. 115.

5. Jeremias, p. 115 and *The Eucharistic Words of Jesus*, pp. 20f.

6. E.g., Jeremias, *New Testament Theology*, pp. 114–116.

7. Vermes, p. 69.

8. Vermes, *The Dead Sea Scrolls*, p. 229.

9. See Jeremias, *The Parables of Jesus*, pp. 126–127, where he argues that love here means gratitude.

10. Schillebeeckx, p. 201.

## 6. THE "KINGDOM" OF GOD

1. The use of *euaggelion* in Mk 1:15; 8:35; 10:29; 13:10 par; 14:9 par, is secondary. Cf. Joachim Jeremias, *New Testament Theology*, p. 134; Edward Schillebeeckx, *Jesus*, pp. 87–88.

2. Jeremias, p. 9.

3. See the thorough research of Richard D. Hiers in *The Kingdom of God in the Synoptic Tradition*.

4. Jeremias, pp. 100–101.

5. S. Aalen, " 'Reign' and 'House' in the Kingdom of God in the Gospels" in *New Testament Studies* (1962), 215–240; Gaston, pp. 231–237. For the idea of *basileia* as reign or ruling power see chapter 10, pp. 83ff, below.

6. Lk 11:5–8; 12:42–46 par; 16:1–8; 17:7–10; Mt 20:1–15; 21:28–31; 25:14–30.

7. Lk 11:15–32; 12:36–38; 14:7–10; Mt 22:1–10 par; 22:11–13; 25:1–12.

8. E. Lohmeyer, *Kultus und Evangelium*, Göttingen, 1942, pp. 72–73.

9. Q Flor 1:1–13; 1QS 5:5–7; 8:1–10; 9:3–6.

10. See chapter 10, p. 83.

## 7. THE "KINGDOM" AND MONEY

1. But see Joachim Jeremias, *The Parables of Jesus*, p. 195.
2. Charles H. Dodd, *The Founder of Christianity*, p. 132.
3. Origen, *In Matthaeum* 15:14; Jeremias, *Unknown Sayings of Jesus*, p. 34.
4. Jeremias, p. 33.

## 8. THE "KINGDOM" AND PRESTIGE

1. J. Duncan M. Derrett, *Law in the New Testament*, p. 40; see also pp. 42, 73.
2. 1QS 2:19–25; 5:23–24; 6:8–13; 1QSa 1:16, 23; 2:11–16; 1QM 2:1–14. For convenient reference see Geza Vermes, *Dead Sea Scrolls*, pp. 74, 80, 81, 119, 120, 121, 125 and see his comment on p. 28.
3. 1QS 15:15; 1QSa 2:4–10 or see Vermes, pp. 109, 120
4. 1QSa 1:16 or Vermes, p. 119.
5. The early Church no doubt exaggerated Jesus' opposition to the Pharisees because of its conflict with them. This is reflected in the gospels, especially in Matthew. Nevertheless Jesus' indignation about hypocrisy as such can hardly have been invented by the early Church.
6. The scholarly and unbiased monogram of S. Légasse has now established this beyond any possible doubt—*Jésus et l'Enfant.*
7. Légasse, p. 106
8. Légasse (p. 118) has shown that the "little flock" meant originally the poor or lower classes. The fact that the early Christians understood themselves to be the little ones (e.g., Mt 10:42), just as they understood themselves to be the poor in spirit (Mt 5:3), confirms the fact that Jesus must have said that the "kingdom" belongs only to the poor and the oppressed and to those who identify themselves with the poor and the oppressed—the little ones.
9. Légasse, p. 118.
10. If the Aramaic word behind this is *sabra*, then the meaning is possibly "the stupid or retarded"! See Légasse, p. 185.
11. Derrett, *Jesus's Audience*, p. 31.

## 9. THE "KINGDOM" AND SOLIDARITY

1. J. Duncan M. Derrett, *Jesus's Audience*, pp. 39–52.
2. Derrett, p. 39.
3. Derrett, p. 39.

4. 1QS 1:9–10; 2:1–9; 9:16, 22; cf. also 4:5; 7:1. For easy reference see Geza Vermes, pp. 72, 73, 88; cf. also 76, 103.

5. 31:29.

6. To come to Jesus or to follow him is to accompany him into the "kingdom." Becoming a disciple is an alternative way of speaking about entering into the "kingdom."

7. Cf. Mt 10:37.

8. Vermes, *Jesus the Jew*, pp. 33–34; David Flusser, *Jesus*, pp. 20–24; Adolf Holl, *Jesus in Bad Company*, pp. 68–70.

9. Cf. Mk 3:12; Jn 7:5 with 1 Cor 9:5; 15:7; Gal 1:19; 2:9; Jude 1.

10. Compare Mk 3:35 par. The same point is made in John 2:1–10. As John sees it, the favor he does for his mother is not based upon biological motherhood, not based upon what she has "to do with" him.

11. For the genuineness and original meaning of Mt 25:40, 45, despite the secondary nature of the parable, see Légasse, pp. 88–93; Jeremias, *The Parables of Jesus*, pp. 208–209.

12. In *Rabbinic Literature and Gospel Teaching*, pp. 103f.

13. Günther Bornkamm, *Jesus of Nazareth*, p. 115.

14. Joachim Jeremias, *Jesus' Promise to the Nations*, p. 12.

15. Eta Linnemann, p. 54.

## 10. THE "KINGDOM" AND POWER

1. K. L. Schmidt et al., *Basileia*, London, 1957, p. 32.

2. E.g., Lk 6:20; 12:32; 19:12, 15; 22:29; Acts 1–6; 1 Cor 4:20; 6:9, 10; 15:24; Heb 12:28; Rev 1:9; 17:12, 17; Dan 7:18, 22, 27.

3. Cf. 1 Sam 2:4, 5, 8.

4. This is an unmistakable correction of Dan 7:14, cf. Lloyd Gaston, *No Stone on Another*, p. 395.

5. That is to say, what we would call secular and what we would call religious. The Jews made no such distinctions. See chapter 13.

6. See the interesting case of Jesus' words to the man who was plowing on the sabbath, which Codex D adds after Luke 6:5. The text can be found in a footnote in the Jerusalem Bible and a commentary can be found in Joachim Jeremias, *Unknown Sayings of Jesus*, pp. 49–54.

7. See p. 130.

## 11. A NEW TIME

1. Gerhard von Rad, *The Message of the Prophets*, p. 77; cf. also Thorlief Boman, *Hebrew Thought Compared with Greek*, Eng. trans.

Philadelphia: Westminster Press, 1961; London, 1960, pp. 139–143.

2. Boman, pp. 149–150.

3. Boman, pp. 147–149.

4. Von Rad, p. 91.

5. Von Rad, p. 93.

6. It may however have some analogies with God's previous acts, cf. Von Rad, p. 93.

7. Von Rad, p. 91.

8. Von Rad, p. 101; cf. also p. 252.

9. Von Rad, p. 100.

10. Von Rad, p. 83.

11. Dan 2:21.

12. Gn 6:6; Jer 26:3, 13, 19; Joel 2:13–19; Amos 5:15; 7:5–6; Jonah 3:9, 10; 4:2; Zech 8:11, 14–15, 19.

13. Cullmann's idea that there is a special biblical doctrine or revelation about the meaning of time which can be discovered by analyzing the biblical words for time (*Christ and Time*) has been successfully refuted by James Barr in *Biblical Words for Time, passim* but especially pp. 155ff. My concern has been to show that time in the Bible is being thought of as a quality rather than a quantity.

14. Luke therefore also understands the "until" of 16:16 as inclusive of John (see Joachim Jeremias, *New Testament Theology*, pp. 46–47). Matthew follows Mark's division but he is not as fully aware of the qualitative differences. He makes John preach the same message as Jesus: "Repent for the kingdom of God is near" (3:2; 4:17).

In the parables Matthew emphasizes the element of judgment and punishment in a way which was more typical of John's time than Jesus' time. And in 11:13 (the verse which is parallel to Lk 16:16) he understands "until" as exclusive of John. I cannot agree with Jeremias here when he concludes that Matthew was right and Luke wrong (p. 47). The time of salvation began with Jesus, not John.

15. Norman Perrin, *Rediscovering the Teaching of Jesus*, p. 89.

16. Heinz Zahrnt, *What Kind of God?*, Eng. trans. Minneapolis: Augsburg, 1972; London, 1971, pp. 55–61.

17. Nothing was more typical of the Hebrew's Creator God than to do new and unprecedented things, to create means to do something new and unprecedented. See Ex 34:10; Nm 16:30; Ps 50:12; 103:30; Is 4:5; 43:19; 48:7; 65:17; 66:22; Jer 31:22; Hab 1:5.

18. His well-known article, *"Abba,"* has been translated into English as chapter 1 of *The Prayers of Jesus*. For a summary of his views on the subject see *The Central Message of the New Testament*, pp. 9–30, or *New Testament Theology*, vol. 1, pp. 61–67.

## 12. THE COMING OF THE "KINGDOM"

1. However Jesus does seem to have said that he would *"build* a new Temple" (Mk 14:58 parr; Jn 2:19); see Lloyd Gaston, *No Stone on Another*, pp. 242–243. But it is interesting that Mark found it necessary to add that it would be a Temple "not made by human hands," which surely means not only that the new Temple would be a community but also that it is God, not human beings, who would build it in and through Jesus.

2. The text at Lk 18:8 would seem to contradict this: "When the son of man comes, will he find any faith on earth?" But the reference here is not to the coming of the "kingdom" but to the coming of the catastrophe or the judgment (see pp. 104-5). Moreover the text is secondary (Gaston, p. 353).

3. The priest-sociologist Andrew M. Greeley, whose approach has enabled him to see the wood despite the overgrowth of trees in the world of New Testament scholarship, has emphasized this point (*The Jesus Myth*, pp. 48–49).

4. Eta Linnemann, pp. 101–104.

5. Gaston, pp. 426–428.

6. See pp. 145–146.

7. Gaston, pp. 422–426.

8. See p. 92.

9. Gaston, pp. 41–60.

10. Gaston, pp. 53–60.

11. Joachim Rohde, *Rediscovering the Teaching of the Evangelists*, pp. 48–49, 55, 107–109.

## 13. POLITICS AND RELIGION

1. Robert Eisler, *Jesous Basileus ou Basileusas*; Samuel G. F. Brandon, *Jesus and the Zealots*; Joel Carmichael, *The Death of Jesus*.

2. P. Feine, *Eine vorkanonische Überliefering des Lukas*, Gotha, 1891; B. H. Sheeter, *The Four Gospels*, London, 1924, pp. 201–222; Vincent Taylor, *Behind the Third Gospel*, Oxford: Clarendon Press, 1926; H. Sahlin, *Der Messias und das Gottesvolk*, Uppsala, 1945; Lloyd Gaston, *No Stone on Another*, pp. 243–256.

3. The Greek word is "eagle" (*aetos*) not "vulture" (*gups*) although it is doubtful whether any distinction was made in Aramaic. The eagle was the Roman military symbol, here seen as indistinguishable from a vulture which devours carrion. See Gaston, p. 353.

4. Alan Richardson, *The Political Christ*, p. 47. One of the first things the Zealots did after overthrowing the Romans in 66 C.E. was to issue new coins—coins inscribed "For the Liberation of Zion" and "Freedom of Zion." See Brandon, *Jesus and the Zealots*, p. 353.

5. "Capitalism–Socialism: A Theological Crux" in *Concilium*, January 1974, p. 118.

6. Joachim Jeremias, *The Parables of Jesus*, p. 139.

7. There is a very similar parable in the Jerusalem Talmud (*circa* 325 C.E.). But the all-important difference is that in the rabbinical parable "justice" is safeguarded by the fact that the laborer who worked for only two hours is said to have done more work in that time than the others had done all day. See Jeremias, pp. 138–139.

8. See Brandon, pp. 43–44.

9. The word *proagousin* has an exclusive sense (instead of you) and not a temporal sense (before you), according to Jeremias, p. 125.

10. J. Duncan M. Derrett, pp. 187–191. See also Jeremias, *New Testament Theology*, pp. 111–112.

## 14. THE INCIDENT IN THE TEMPLE

1. Mark builds up the opposition of the scribes, Pharisees and Herodians to Jesus (2:6, 16, 24; 3:2, 6, 22; 7:1–2; 8:11, 15). Then, after several references to Jesus' withdrawal from the crowds and from the villages of Galilee (7:24, 31; 8:22, 27), he brings the first part of his gospel to a climax with Peter's so-called "confession" of Jesus' messiahship (8:27–30), which is followed by the instructions to his disciples about his impending death (8:31–32; 9:30–32; 10:33–34) and by the beginning of his journey to Jerusalem (10:1, 32, 46). Matthew follows Mark. He sees the opposition as that of the Pharisees and Sadducees rather than the Pharisees and Herodians (16:1, 6, 11, 12) and yet he maintains that the reason for Jesus' withdrawal was Herod's execution of John the Baptist (14:13). Luke also follows Mark, although for him the principal opponents are simply the scribes and Pharisees (e.g., 5:17, 21, 30; 6:2). On the other hand, in Luke it is the Pharisees who warn Jesus that Herod wants to kill him and who therefore advise him to withdraw (13:31). But according to Luke, Jesus was not concerned about Herod's threats because he knew that he must die in Jerusalem (13:32–33). Hence the long journey to Jerusalem (9:51; 10:38; 13:22; 17:11; 18:35; 19:1, 11, 28). John is independent of Mark. He is not particularly interested in the various "parties" among the leaders of Israel. Jesus' opponents are simply the Jews (e.g., 2:18; 5:10, 16, 18; 6:41, 52) or the Pharisees (e.g., 7:32; 8:13; 9:14, 15, 40). The turning

point for John and the reason for Jesus' withdrawal was the decision of the Sanhedrin that Jesus must die (11:45–54).

2. "L'Expulsion des Marchands du Temple" in *New Testament Studies* 15 (1968–9), pp. 1–22 and Etienne Trocmé, *Jesus as Seen by His Contemporaries*, pp. 110–115.

3. Apart from the Gospel of John, see Mk 10:47; 11:1–6; 14:3, 13–15; 15:43.

4. Joel Carmichael, pp. 111–133; Samuel G. F. Brandon, *Jesus and the Zealots*, pp. 331–336, 350–351.

5. Cf. Lloyd Gaston, *No Stone on Another*, p. 85.

6. Joachim Jeremias, *Jerusalem in the Time of Jesus*, pp. 48–49.

7. Jeremias, pp. 33–34.

8. Jeremias, p. 134.

9. Gaston, p. 102.

10. See note 4 above.

11. See Oscar Cullmann, *The State in the New Testament*, pp. 31–34.

## 15. THE TEMPTATION TO VIOLENCE

1. Psalms of Solomon 17.

2. Psalms of Solomon 18.

3. Ferdinand Hahn, *The Titles of Jesus in Christology*, pp. 136–138; Vermes, *Jesus the Jew*, pp. 130–134.

4. Mk 9:41; 14:62 (but cf. Mt 26:64; Lk 22:70 and Mk 15:2; Mt 27:11; Lk 23:3; Jn 18:37); Mt 11:2; Jn 4:25–26 (but cf. Jn 7:26–27, 31, 40–44; 10:24–26, 38).

5. Mk 1:24–25, 34; 3:12; 8:30; Lk 4:41; see also Mk 1:44; 5:43; 7:36; 8:26; 9:9; Mt 9:30.

6. Judas the Galilean, their founder, had been killed and his followers had scattered (Acts 5:37). Judas's sons were probably too young to reorganize and lead the movement at this time. Two of them, Jacob and Simon, turn up again around 46–48 C.E., when they are captured and crucified; while another son Menahen led the revolt of 66 C.E.; and finally a descendant named Eleazar was the leader of the Zealots on Masada in 73 C.E. See Samuel G. F. Brandon, *Jesus and the Zealots*, pp. 52, 103, 131–133.

7. Martin Hengel, *Victory over Violence*, pp. 55, 61, 64–65; Floyd V. Filson, *A New Testament History*, Philadelphia: Westminster Press, 1964; London, 1965, p. 27.

## 16. THE ROLE OF SUFFERING AND DEATH

1. Josephus, *Antiquities* 14:67.

2. *Antiquities* 7:416–419; see Samuel G. F. Brandon, *The Trial of Jesus of Nazareth*, p. 57, 1.

3. W. H. C. Frend, *Martyrdom and Persecution in the Early Church*, pp. 57–58.

4. Frend, pp. 45, 57, 59; Joachim Jeremias, *New Testament Theology*, pp. 287–288.

5. Jürgen Moltmann, "Die Gekruisigde God" in *N. G. Teologiese Tydskrif*, March 1973, p. 110.

6. For riddles as a characteristic of Jesus' style see Jeremias, pp. 30–31.

7. This is precisely what John (12:25) has done.

8. Like the dead who must be left to bury their dead (Mt 8:22 par).

9. J. Roloff has argued in great detail and very convincingly that the original meaning of Jesus' death was service and that this may very well have been Jesus' own understanding of his death—"Anfänge der soteriologischen Deutung des Todes Jesu (Mk 10:45 und Lk 22:27)," *New Testament Studies*, pp. 38–64. Schillebeeckx has taken the argument a step further and shown that Jesus himself must have understood his death as a service to humankind—*Jesus*, pp. 251–256.

10. Jeremias, pp. 130, 291, 293.

11. It should be noted that the awakening of faith also makes God's forgiveness effective in a person. Jesus says to the woman who was a sinner: "Your faith has saved you" (from your sins) (Lk 7:50). It follows that one of the results of Jesus' death would be the forgiveness of sin. This is the sense in which Jesus' death may be called an atonement for sin. Jesus did not have to placate an angry God who was unwilling to forgive. God is always willing to forgive and to forgive unconditionally. Jesus' death reveals this and awakens our faith in it, thereby allowing God's forgiveness to transform our lives.

12. Mk 8:31 par; 9:31 par; 10:33–34 par; 10:45; Mt 26:2; Lk 17:25; 24:7.

13. Jeremias has reduced these "predictions" to the basic and original riddle: "The man will be handed over to men"—Jeremias, pp. 281–283, 295–296.

14. Jeremias, pp. 108–110; Lloyd Gaston, p. 420; Frend, p. 88; Thomas W. Manson, *The Teachings of Jesus*, p. 231.

15. Jeremias, p. 285; Gaston, p. 415; Edward Schillebeeckx, *Jesus*, pp. 526–532; E. L. Bode, "On the Third Day according to the Scriptures," *The Bible Today* 48 (1970), 3297–3303.

16. C. F. Evans, *Resurrection and the New Testament*, pp. 30–33.

## 17. THE MAN WHO EMERGES

1. J. Duncan M. Derrett, *Law in the New Testament*, p. 13.

2. Mk 4:41 parr; 6:2 parr; 6:14–16 parr; 8:27–30 parr; 14:61 parr;

15:2 parr; 15:39 parr; Lk 7:16–17; Jn 7:12, 15, 40–41; 8:54; 10:19–21, 24. The form and wording of these questions may come from the early Church but in substance they express the curiosity of Jesus' contemporaries.

3. Geza Vermes, *Jesus the Jew*, pp. 160–168, 186.

4. Vermes, p. 176.

5. Mk 8:38 parr; 13:26 parr; 14:62 parr; Mt 19:28 par; 24:27, 37, 44 par.

6. For example, Vermes, pp. 169–186; Norman Perrin, *Rediscovering the Teaching of Jesus*, pp. 164–199.

7. Ernst Käsemann, *Essays in New Testament Themes*, pp. 37–38; Ernst Fuchs, *Studies of the Historical Jesus*, pp. 36–37; Günther Bornkamm, pp. 173–174; Joachim Jeremias, *New Testament Theology*, pp. 250–252; Jeremias, *The Parables of Jesus*, p. 132; Wolfhart Pannenberg, *Jesus, God and Man*, pp. 53–65.

8. Käsemann, pp. 144–145.

9. Pannenberg, p. 55; James M. Robinson, *A New Quest of the Historical Jesus*, *passim* but especially pp. 70–71.

10. E.g., Mk 1:27; 2:10, 28; 4:41; 6:7 and parallels.

11. Eta Linnemann, *Jesus of the Parables* pp. 21–23, 31.

12. Linnemann, p. 40.

13. Jesus recognizes of course that he is a prophet but he does not rely upon the authority which one would have as a prophet. Even if he did experience a calling (see Jeremias, pp. 49–56), or have a vision (see Pannenberg, p. 64), Jesus never appealed to either of these in order to authenticate his words.

14. See p. 45; see also Werner & Lotte Pelz, *God Is No More*, p. 113.

15. Edward Schillebeeckx, *Jesus*, pp. 257–271; Vermes, *Jesus the Jew*, pp. 210–213; Heinz Zahrnt, *What Kind of God?*, p. 163; Jeremias, pp. 67–68.

16. Von Rad, *The Message of the Prophets*, pp. 42, 50, 165–166.

## 18. ON TRIAL

1. Much has been written in recent times about the trial of Jesus and about the motives of the evangelists and their sources in reconstructing the events. For the reader who is not able to wade through the flood of literature on the topic, I would recommend the little book of Gerard S. Sloyan, *Jesus on Trial*, or the article by J. Sobosan, "The Trial of Jesus," *Journal of Ecumenical Studies*, 10.1 (1973), 70–91.

2. Joachim Jeremias, *New Testament Theology*, pp. 278–279. There

was also the possible accusation that he wished to destroy the Temple, but that was never taken very seriously (Mk 14:57–59 par).

3. *Legatio ad Gaium*, 299–305.

4. *Antiquities* 18:55–57.

5. *Antiquities* 18:61–62; *War* 2:175–177.

6. *Antiquities* 18:85–89.

7. *Antiquities* 20:97–99; Acts 5:36.

8. Martin Hengel, *Die Zeloten*, pp. 236–238.

9. *Antiquities* 20:169–172.

10. See chapter 2 and Geza Vermes, *Jesus the Jew*, pp. 50–51.

11. Vermes, pp. 51, 144.

12. John's statement at 7:32 expresses this idea very accurately: "Hearing that rumors like this about him" (i.e., that he might be the Messiah) "were spreading among the people, the Pharisees" (!) "sent the Temple police to arrest him."

13. Paul Winter, *On the Trial of Jesus*, p. 39.

14. Genesis Rabbah 94:9 and compare the story of Sheba in 2 Samuel 20. See Merx, *Das Evangelium des Johannes*, pp. 298–299; D. Daube, *Collaboration with Tyranny in Rabbinic Law*, New York and London: Oxford University Press, 1966, *passim*; Vermes, *Jesus the Jew*, pp. 50–51. E. Bammel's arguments against the idea that what we have here is a case of extradition are not convincing (*The Trial of Jesus*, pp. 26–30).

15. For the historicity of Jesus' silence see Edward Schillebeeckx, *Jesus*, p. 315; Etienne Trocmé, pp. 75–77.

16. *Peirasmos* means temptation, test or trial.

17. This is not to say that there were no innocent people who continued to believe in him and to stand by him to the end. We are told that Mary and "the beloved disciple" and several of the women were at the foot of the cross (Mk 15:40 parr; Jn 19:25–27). But they were not the ones who were tested by these events. Of all those who were put to the test—Jesus, Caiaphas, Pilate, Judas, Peter, etc.—only Jesus survived, paradoxically by dying.

### 19. FAITH IN JESUS

1. Christian Duquoc, "Yes to Jesus–No to God and the Church," *Concilium*, October 1974, 17–30.

2. Edward Schillebeeckx, *Jesus*, p. 545.

3. Gustavo Gutiérrez, *A Theology of Liberation*, p. 10; Hugo Assmann, *Theology for a Nomad Church*, p. 80.

4. Gutiérrez, p. 10; Assmann, pp. 76–77, 81, 122; Schillebeeckx, *God the Future of Man*, pp. 35, 182–186.

5. T. Paul Verghese, *The Freedom of Man*, Philadelphia: Westminster Press, 1972, p. 57.

# BIBLIOGRAPHY

Alves, Rubem. *Tomorrow's Child: Imagination, Creativity and the Rebirth of Culture.* Eng. trans. London: SCM, 1972.

Assmann, Hugo. *Theology for a Nomad Church.* Eng. trans. U.S. ed. Maryknoll, NY: Orbis Books, 1978; *Practical Theology of Liberation.* U.K. ed. London: Search, 1975.

Bammel, E. (ed.). *The Trial of Jesus.* London: SCM, 1970.

Barr, James. *Biblical Words for Time.* Naperville, IL: Allenson, 1962; London: SCM, 1962.

Barrett, Charles K. *The Holy Spirit and the Gospel Tradition.* New York: Macmillan, 1947; London: SPCK, 1947.

Batey, Richard. *Jesus and the Poor.* New York: Harper & Row, 1972.

Betz, Otto. *What Do We Know about Jesus?* Philadelphia: Westminster, 1968; London: SCM, 1968.

Blinzler, Josef. *The Trial of Jesus.* Eng. trans. Westminster, MD: Newman Press, 1959.

Boff, Leonardo. *Jesus Christ Liberator.* Eng. trans. Maryknoll, NY: Orbis Books, 1978; London: SPCK, 1979.

Bornkamm, Günther. *Jesus of Nazareth.* Eng. trans. New York: Harper & Row, 1975; London: Hodder & Stoughton, 1960.

Brandon, Samuel G. F. *The Fall of Jerusalem and the Christian Church.* London, 1951, 2nd ed. 1957.

Brandon, Samuel G. F. *Jesus and the Zealots.* New York: Scribner's, 1967; Manchester: Manchester University Press, 1967.

Brandon, Samuel G. F. *The Trial of Jesus of Nazareth.* Chelsea, MI: Scarborough House, 1979; London: Batsford, 1968.

Bultmann, Rudolf. *The History of the Synoptic Tradition.* New York: Harper & Row, 1968; London: Blackwell, 1963.

Cadbury, Henry J. *The Peril of Modernizing Jesus.* New York: Macmillan, 1937; London: SPCK, 1962.

Carmichael, Joel. *The Death of Jesus.* New York, 1963; London: Gollancz, 1963.

Conzelmann, Hans. *Jesus.* Eng. trans. Philadelphia: Fortress, 1973.

Conzelmann, Hans. *The Theology of Saint Luke.* Eng. trans. New York: Harper, 1961; London: Faber, 1960.

Cullmann, Oscar. *Christ and Time.* Eng. trans. Philadelphia: Westminster, 1964; London: SCM, 1965.

Cullmann, Oscar. *The Christology of the New Testament*, rev. ed. Eng. trans. Philadelphia: Westminster John Knox, 1980; London: SCM, 1968.

Cullmann, Oscar. *Jesus and the Revolutionaries.* Eng. trans. New York: Harper & Row, 1970.

Cullmann, Oscar. *The State in the New Testament.* Eng. trans. New York: Scribner's, 1956; London: SCM, 1962.

Davies, William D. *Christian Origins and Judaism.* Philadelphia: Westminster, 1973; London: Darton, Longman & Todd, 1962.

Davies, William D. *The Setting of the Sermon on the Mount.* New York and Cambridge: Cambridge University Press, 1964.

Derrett, J. Duncan M. *Jesus's Audience: The Social and Psychological Environment in Which He Worked.* New York: Seabury Press, 1974; London: Darton, Longman & Todd, 1973.

Derrett, J. Duncan M. *Law in the New Testament.* London: Darton, Longman & Todd, 1970.

Dodd, Charles H. "The Fall of Jerusalem and the 'Abomination of Desolation'," *Journal of Roman Studies* 37 (1947), 47–54.

Dodd, Charles H. *The Founder of Christianity.* New York and London: Macmillan, 1970.

Dodd, Charles H. *The Parables of the Kingdom.* New York: Harper & Row, 1961; London: Nisbet, 1955.

Duquoc, Christian. *Jésus, Homme Libre.* Paris: Cerf, 1974.

Ebeling, Gerhard. *Word and Faith.* Eng. trans. Philadelphia: Fortress, 1963; London: SCM, 1963.

Eisler, Robert. *Jesous Basileus ou Basileusas.* Heidelberg, 1928–30.

Elliott-Binns, Leonard E. *Galilean Christianity.* London: SCM, 1956.

Evans, C. F. *Resurrection and the New Testament.* London: SCM, 1970.

Flusser, David. *Jesus.* Eng. trans. New York: Herder & Herder, 1969.

Frend, W. H. C. *Martyrdom and Persecution in the Early Church.* New York: New York University Press, 1967; Oxford: Oxford University Press, 1965.

Fuchs, Ernst. *Studies of the Historical Jesus.* Eng. trans. Naperville, IL: Allenson, 1964; London: SCM, 1964.

Fuller, Reginald H. *The Foundations of New Testament Christology.* New York: Scribner's, 1965; London: Fontana, 1969.

Fuller, Reginald H. *Interpreting the Miracles.* Philadelphia: Westminster, 1963; London: SCM, 1966.

Gaston, Lloyd. *No Stone on Another.* Leiden: E. J. Brill, 1970.

Greeley, Andrew M. *The Jesus Myth.* New York: Doubleday, 1971; London: Search, 1972.

Gutiérrez, Gustavo. *A Theology of Liberation.* Rev. ed. Eng. trans. Maryknoll, NY: Orbis Books, 1988; London: SCM, 1989.

Hahn, Ferdinand. *The Titles of Jesus in Christology.* Eng. trans. New York: World Pub. Co., 1969; London: Lutterworth, 1969.

Hengel, Martin. *Die Zeloten.* Leiden: E. J. Brill, 1961.

Hengel, Martin. *Victory over Violence: Jesus and the Revolutionists.* Eng. trans. Philadelphia: Fortress, 1973; London: SPCK, 1975.

Hiers, Richard H. *The Kingdom of God in the Synoptic Tradition.* Gainesville: The University of Florida Press, 1979.

Holl, Adolf. *Jesus in Bad Company.* Eng. trans. New York: Holt, Rinehart & Winston, 1973; London: Collins, 1972.

Jeremias, Joachim. *The Central Message of the New Testament.* Eng. trans. Ann Arbor: University of Michigan Microfilms; London: SCM, 1965.

Jeremias, Joachim. *The Eucharistic Words of Jesus.* Eng. trans. New York: Scribner's, 1966; London: SCM, 1966.

Jeremias, Joachim. *Jerusalem in the Time of Jesus.* Eng. trans. Minneapolis: Augsburg Fortress, 1975; London: SCM, 1969.

Jeremias, Joachim. *Jesus' Promise to the Nations.* Eng. trans. Philadelphia: Fortress, 1982; London: SCM, 1958.

Jeremias, Joachim. *New Testament Theology, Vol 1: The Proclamation of Jesus.* Eng. trans. New York: Macmillan, 1971; London: SCM, 1971.

Jeremias, Joachim. *The Parables of Jesus.* Eng. trans. New York: Macmillan, 1972; London: SCM, 1963.

Jeremias, Joachim. *The Prayers of Jesus.* Eng. trans. Minneapolis: Augsburg Fortress, 1978; London: SCM, 1967.

Jeremias, Joachim. *Unknown Sayings of Jesus.* Eng. trans. New York: Scribner's, 1966; London: SPCK, 1958.

Käsemann, Ernst. *Essays on New Testament Themes.* Eng. trans. Philadelphia: Fortress, 1982; London: SCM, 1964.

Käsemann, Ernst. *Jesus Means Freedom.* Eng. trans. Philadelphia: Fortress, 1970; London: SCM, 1969.

Keck, Leander E. *A Future for the Historical Jesus.* Philadelphia: Fortress, 1981; London: SCM, 1972.

Le Moyne, J. *Les Sadducéens.* Paris, 1972.

Légasse, S. *Jésus et l'Enfant: "Enfants," "Petits" et "simples" dans la Tradition Synoptique.* Paris, 1969.

Léon-Dufour, Xavier. *The Gospels and the Jesus of History.* Eng. trans. New York: Doubleday, 1971; London: Collins, 1968.

Linnemann, Eta. *Jesus of the Parables: Introduction and Exposition.* Eng. trans. New York: Harper & Row, 1967; London: SPCK, 1966.

Manson, Thomas W. *The Sayings of Jesus.* New York: Cambridge University Press, 1963; London: SCM, 1931.

Manson, Thomas W. *The Teachings of Jesus.* Grand Rapids, MI: Eerdmans, 1979; Cambridge: Cambridge University Press, 1935.

Marxsen, Willi. *Mark the Evangelist: Studies on the Redaction History of the Gospel.* Eng. trans. Nashville, TN: Abingdon, 1977.

Mitton, C. Leslie. *Jesus: The Fact Behind the Faith.* Grand Rapids, MI: Eerdmans, 1974; London: Mowbrays, 1975.

Moltmann, Jürgen. *Theology of Hope.* New York: Harper & Row, 1976; London: SCM, 1967.

Moltmann, Jürgen. *Theology and Joy.* London: SCM, 1974.

Montefiore, Hugh. *Can Man Survive?* London: Fontana, 1970.

Pannenberg, Wolfhart. *Jesus, God and Man.* 2nd ed. Eng. trans. Philadelphia: Westminster, 1977; London: SCM, 1970.

Pannenberg, Wolfhart. *Theology and the Kingdom of God.* Philadelphia: Westminster, 1977.

Pelz, Werner and Lotte. *God Is No More.* Philadelphia: Lippincott, 1964; London: Gollancz, 1963.

Perrin, Norman. *The Kingdom of God in the Teaching of Jesus.* Philadelphia: Westminster, 1963; London: SCM, 1963.

Perrin, Norman. *Rediscovering the Teaching of Jesus.* New York: Harper & Row, 1967; London: SCM, 1967.

Richardson, Alan. *The Political Christ.* Philadelphia: Westminster, 1973; London: SCM, 1973.

Robinson, James M. *A New Quest of the Historical Jesus.* Naperville, IL: Allenson, 1959; London: SCM, 1959.

Rohde, Joachim. *Rediscovering the Teaching of the Evangelists.* Eng. trans. Philadelphia: Westminster, 1968; London: SCM, 1969.

Russell, D. S. *The Method and Message of Jewish Apocalyptic.* London: SCM, 1964.

Schillebeeckx, Edward. *God, the Future of Man.* Eng. trans. New York: Sheed & Ward, 1968; London: Sheed & Ward, 1969.

Schillebeeckx, Edward. *Jesus: An Experiment in Christology.* Eng. trans. New York: Crossroad, 1982; London: SCM, 1982.

Scobie, Charles H. H. *John the Baptist.* Philadelphia: Fortress, 1964; London: SCM, 1964.

Sloyan, Gerard S. *Jesus on Trial.* Philadelphia: Fortress, 1973.

Sölle, Dorothee. *Christ the Representative.* Eng. trans. Philadelphia: Fortress, 1967; London: SCM, 1967.

Trocmé, Etienne. *Jesus as Seen by His Contemporaries.* Eng. trans. Philadelphia: Westminster, 1973; London: SCM, 1973.

Vermes, Geza. *The Dead Sea Scrolls in English.* New York: Penguin, 1968; London: Penguin, 1962.

Vermes, Geza. *Jesus the Jew: A Historian's Reading of the Gospels.* Minneapolis: Augsburg Fortress, 1981; London: Collins, 1973.

Von Rad, Gerhard. *The Message of the Prophets.* Eng. trans. New York: Harper & Row, 1972; London: SCM, 1968.

Winter, Paul. *On the Trial of Jesus.* 2nd ed. New York: De Gruyter, 1974.

# INDEX

*193*